RMS QUEEN MARY

RMS QUEEN MARY

101 Questions and Answers about the Great Transatlantic Liner

David Ellery

CONWAY

Title spread: Lit both by dockside floodlights and by her own lights, *Queen Mary* being fitted out at John Brown's yard, Clydebank, on 5 March 1936. HM King George V had visited the ship earlier in the day.
Endpapers: Deck plans and inboard profile of *Queen Mary* as originally constructed. (*Shipbuilding and Shipping Record*, 14 May 1936)

To Sharon

First published in Great Britain in 2006 by Conway,
an imprint of Anova Books, 151 Freston Road, London W10 6TH
www.anovabooks.com

Distributed in North America by Casemate Publishing
2114 Darby Road
Havertown, PA 19083, USA

British Library Cataloguing in Publication Data:
A catalogue record for this book is available from the British Library

Library of Congress Cataloguing in Publication Data Available

ISBN 10: 1 84486 033 7   ISBN 13: 9 781844 860333

Edited by Nicki Marshall
Design and layout by Stephen Dent
Printed in China

Contents

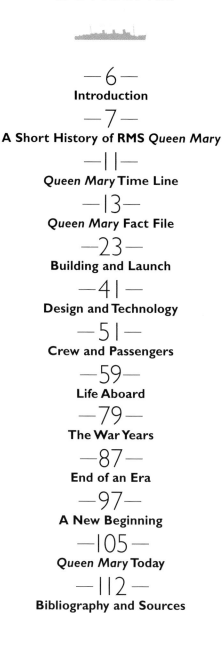

Introduction

I never cease to be surprised (and greatly pleased) by the amount of interest and enthusiasm the 'old girl' *Queen Mary* still attracts. And yet I shouldn't be. Like a valuable antique, the liner becomes just a little more intrinsically valuable with every year that passes. But unlike an antique, no-one is likely to discover another one just like it in their attic. *Queen Mary* is unique. In *101 Questions and Answers* I have tried to give a flavour of what made the ship special during her ocean-going days, her historical context, and a balanced view of the ship today and her possible future. As someone who speaks regularly about *Queen Mary* and other historic ships, some of the questions I'm most frequently asked are included here. But the most popular one isn't among the 101, so I'll answer it now... 'How did you first become interested in the ship?' My answer is simple: in 1990, while working as a freelance journalist I went to Los Angeles on assignment. Between celebrity interviews I visited the tourist attractions, including *Queen Mary*. It was a half-day tour – too short, but long enough for me to be captivated.

Since then I have stayed aboard on many occasions, had the privilege of delving into the extensive archive, and continue to be involved in many media projects concerning the ship. Whenever I return I feel 'at home'. It's a sentiment I've heard from many a former passenger and crew member. The ship may not go anywhere except back in time, but she's now a destination in her own right.

David Ellery

Acknowledgements

Grateful thanks to Joseph Prevratil, the RMS Foundation Inc., Martha Chacon, Lawrence Hole, John Lee, Stephen Dent, Nicki Marshall, Marine Art Posters and everyone who has helped in the compilation of this book and allowed images to be included.

Except where otherwise credited, all images are from the archives of the *Queen Mary* and Conway Maritime Press. The silhouette of *Queen Mary* is based on a drawing by John Bowen.

A Short History of RMS *Queen Mary*

In May 1936 RMS *Queen Mary* embarked on her maiden voyage. Ahead of her lay a 31-year ocean-going career and a list of record-breaking achievements. She was to become a favourite with stars and royalty, influence the course of the Second World War and become an icon of 1930s glamour…

Building Britain's first liner over 1,000 feet (305 metres) in length was a huge endeavour that captured the interest of the public and international press. Work began on 1 December 1930, but just months before the expected launch construction came to an abrupt halt due to the Great Depression. Nearly 14,000 people employed directly and indirectly on the project were out of work.

For the next 27 months the half-finished ship languished on the stocks at the yard in Clydebank, dominating the skyline and accumulating an incredible 130 tons of rust – an indication of the vessel's vast size. Finally, a solution was found. With the aid of a Government loan work resumed. It was an enormous morale boost for the people of Britain, and the first step in the nation's recovery from recession.

Once the ship was launched, hundreds of craftsmen completed the task of turning the hollow steel hull into a luxurious floating hotel. Throughout Britain and various parts of the British Empire, men and women toiled to produce components that would be scrutinised and utilised by the ship's passengers. First Class travellers were used to gracious living and the new ship would have to cater for their every need. She was opulent and elegant in the extreme. Ten miles of blankets were produced from 16 tons of merino wool; six miles of carpets and rugs were woven for public rooms and staterooms. Additionally, 30,000 sheets and 31,000 pillowcases were produced, along with 200,000 pieces of china and earthenware. Below decks other components were gradually installed, including boilers, turbines and turbo-generators capable of providing 10,000 kilowatts of electricity.

The ship was divided into three classes of accommodation, which varied in opulence, size and location. Originally, these were designated Cabin, Tourist and Third class, but after the Second World War Cunard renamed the classes

First, Cabin and Tourist, which implied even higher levels of luxury. For clarity, except when discussing the class structure, they are referred to in the text as First, Second and Third, as 'Cabin' and 'Tourist' were each used for different classes at different times. The three sections were always quite separate, each class having its own entrance, and gates manned by stewards prevented intermingling and social climbing. There are many stewards who can recall offers of bribes and certain favours for allowing a passenger to 'slip' through to the next class.

The Cunard Line, owner of the new ship, was keen to woo passengers from rival companies and establish *Queen Mary* as the vessel of choice for Atlantic crossings. Interior decor, especially in First Class, was rich: the panelling featured 56 different veneers, which inspired Cunard publicists to coin the term 'the ship of beautiful woods'. The overall effect was enhanced by specially commissioned artwork supplied by over thirty prominent artists of the day.

Following sea trials and a royal tour, which Her Majesty Queen Mary had requested, the ship embarked on her maiden voyage from Southampton on 27 May 1936. Public interest was higher than ever and Britain's new grand vessel received a send-off from a crowd of over a quarter of a million. People lined the shoreline, eager to get a glimpse of Britain's biggest ship. It was hoped the new Cunarder would make a record-breaking crossing and win the prestigious Blue Riband from rival superliner *Normandie* (1935) of the

Queen Mary in her element: crossing the North Atlantic at speed.

French Line. In the event *Queen Mary* was forced to reduce speed due to fog and narrowly missed setting a new time. But a few weeks later she was successful, breaking the record for the fastest round trip across the Atlantic.

The new liner soon earned an enviable reputation for outstanding service. Many passengers, including an array of royalty, politicians and celebrities, returned time and time again. The ship was like a village at sea, able to offer her passengers everything from banks and beauty parlours to a hospital and shops. There was even a resident gardener to tend the numerous potted plants, and a dog-walking service provided by the bell boys. A highlight of the voyage for a select few was the opportunity to dine at 'Table 199', the Captain's table. On one occasion a misunderstanding occurred when a passenger was presented with the coveted invitation. To the amazement of his steward, he turned it down saying: 'I've saved my entire life for this trip, and I'll be blasted if I'll spend it eating with the crew.' But once the prestige of the request became clear, the matter was quickly resolved.

The new superliner was largely the success Cunard had hoped, but for one problem: her ability to roll. Her crew joked she could roll the milk out of a cup of tea, and in the early days before furniture was secured to the decks a great deal of damage occurred; injuries were not uncommon.

By March 1940 things were very different. *Queen Mary* was going to war. Her speed and size made her invaluable as a troop-carrier, and so her luxurious interior fittings were removed and replaced by bunks and extra sanitary facilities to accommodate service personnel. As the Second World War progressed she voyaged to new areas of the world, and her capacity was further increased. On 25 July 1943 she carried an astonishing 16,683 people from New York to Gourock in Scotland, the greatest number to be conveyed on a single voyage, a record that still stands to this day. *Queen Mary* ended her war duties in September 1946, having carried 810,730 troops and steamed nearly 670,000 miles. Churchill paid tribute to both *Queen Mary* and her sistership *Queen Elizabeth*, which put to sea for the first time in March 1940 and also carried troops. It was widely acknowledged that their contribution helped shorten the Second World War significantly.

After a lengthy refit and refurbishment, *Queen Mary* resumed her peacetime duties. The French leviathan *Normandie* had been destroyed by fire during conversion to troop-carrier and the two *Queens*, the fastest and largest passenger ships in the world, now ruled the North Atlantic. It was a reign that continued until the development of travel by passenger jet in the late 1950s.

Life aboard was never quite as carefree as before the war, but passengers, public and celebrity alike, could still enjoy fine cuisine and the opportunity to dance until the small hours. The ship benefited from several modifications made during the post-war refit, and further improvements came in 1958 when stabilizers were fitted. They significantly reduced the rolling action, making even winter crossings much smoother.

But the end was inevitable. The advantages of jet travel resulted in overwhelming competition. In 1966 a First Class return crossing cost around £2,000 for a couple sharing, but by now *Queen Mary* alone was losing £750,000 a year. The decision was made: Cunard's *Queens* were to go.

Queen Mary was the first to be sold. She was purchased by the City of Long Beach in California for $3.45 million (£1.23 million). *Queen Mary* left Southampton for the last time in October 1967 watched by thousands of emotional well-wishers. Some 39 days later the ship arrived at Long Beach and Captain John Treasure Jones gave the order 'Finished with engines' for the last time. As the ship retired, so did her captain. An era was all but over.

However, for Long Beach the adventure was just beginning. The ship would be converted into a floating museum, convention centre and tourist attraction. *Queen Mary* has now been in retirement in the sun on the west coast of America far longer than she was ever at sea. A generation of Californians consider her 'their ship'. It's true to say the liner's new role has been fraught with difficulty for long periods of time. The conversion which commenced virtually on arrival took much longer than first estimated, and budgets soared. But the ship's hull below the water line is still in good shape, much of her 1930s Art Deco interior remains, and in recent years painstaking restoration work has been accomplished. Other exciting projects and developments are earmarked for the future.

As the solitary tangible reminder of the days of travel by superliner, RMS *Queen Mary* is more important now than ever. She is unique, and like a great masterpiece or ancient building, needs to be conserved as part of the world's heritage for generations to come.

Queen Mary Timeline

1926 : Sir Percy Bates (Chairman of Cunard Line) conceives idea of two superliners to operate a transatlantic service

1930 : Work begins on 'Job number 534'

1932 : Work stops due to the Great Depression

1934 : Work is resumed

1934 : Her Majesty Queen Mary launches and names the new ship

1936 : Maiden Voyage

1936 & 1938 : Blue Riband is won

1940 : *Queen Mary* becomes troop-carrier

1942 : Ship collides with HMS *Curacoa*

1943 : New record set for greatest number of people carried on a single voyage

1946 : War duties come to an end, and post-war refit begins

1947 : Post-war maiden voyage and the beginning of the two-ship weekly service conceived 21 years earlier

1949 : Ship is under serious threat due to grounding at Cherbourg

1952 : *Queen Mary* is docked without tugs in New York

1957 : The beginning of the end – airlines attract fifty per cent of the market

1958 : Stabilizers are fitted to *Queen Mary*

1963 : The vessel's first foray into cruising

1967 : Cunard Line tell the captain and crew of the *Queen* liners that their ships are to be withdrawn

1967 : *Queen Mary* leaves Southampton for the last time, bound for Long Beach, California

1971 : The ship is converted and opens as a tourist attraction

1992 : Speculation over the future of the ship, with a suggestion she may be sold or scrapped

1993 : RMS Foundation Inc take over the operation of *Queen Mary* after Long Beach City Council vote unanimously to keep the ship

2001 : Restoration of teak decking

2006 : *Queen Mary* celebrates her 70th anniversary

Queen Mary is put through her paces during sea trials off the Isle of Arran in Scotland, 1936.

Queen Mary Fact File

I ■ How fast was *Queen Mary*?

Queen Mary (1936) and her sistership *Queen Elizabeth* (1940) were designed to replace three ships – *Mauretania*, *Aquitania* and *Berengaria* (1907, 1914, 1913) – working Cunard Line's weekly transatlantic service. Consequently they needed to be larger and faster than their predecessors. *Queen Mary* was designed with a cruising speed of 28.5 knots, which she could easily attain, with plenty of power left in reserve. Before entering service she went through speed trials using the Admiralty Measured Mile, off the Isle of Arran, Scotland. During these trials the new liner unofficially achieved a remarkable 34 knots, nearly 40 mph, which is an impressive speed for a vessel with a gross tonnage of nearly 81,000 tons. The wave caused by the ship was reported to be 12 feet (3.6 metres) high when it hit the shore. Lord Aberconway, chairman of John Brown & Co., *Queen Mary*'s builders, sent a telegram from the ship stating: '…the speed and other trials of the *Queen Mary*, concluding today, have been in every way successful and the performance of the vessel has amply fulfilled our expectations.'

2 ■ How much fuel did *Queen Mary* use?

At the average cruising speed of 28.5 knots the ship burned around 1,000 tons of oil a day but during prolonged periods at higher speeds, like her record-breaking transatlantic runs, consumption increased dramatically to about 1,400 tons per day. This equates to an average 12 feet (3.5 metres) per gallon.

3 ■ How big is the vessel?

Length: 1,019½ feet (310.74 metres)
Width: 118 feet (36 metres)
Height: 237 feet (72.23 metres) – Keel to top of foremast
Gross Tonnage: 80,773 (1936)
                   81,237 (1937 onward)*

* The ship's Gross Tonnage was increased when Engineers' Quarters were added above the Verandah Grill in December 1936.

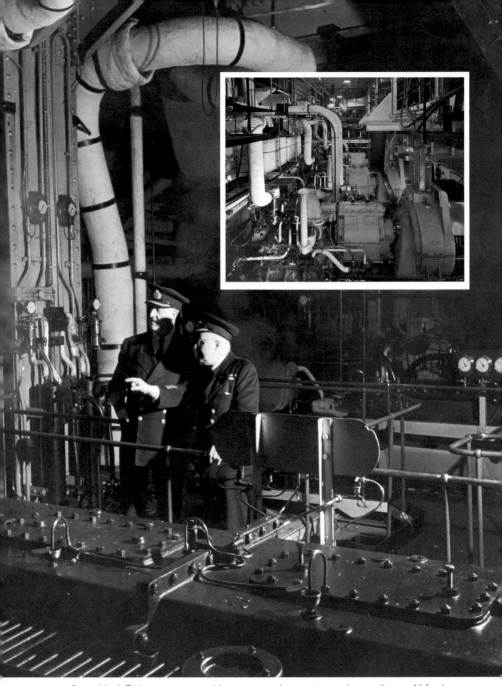

Queen Mary's Turbo-generators could muster enough power to supply a small town. All food preparation like peeling, slicing and dough-mixing, and even de-stoning raisins, was done by machine, so along with refrigeration units, dishwashers and 22 Otis lifts, demand for power was ferocious.

4 ■ How is a ship's gross tonnage measured?

Gross Tonnage is not a weight measurement, but space calculation. It takes into account all enclosed areas of the vessel, including machinery space and capacity occupied by fuel, cargo and people. The Gross Tonnage is calculated by dividing the ship's total capacity in cubic feet by 100.

5 ■ What is *Queen Mary's* draft?

Her draft (amount of the vessel below the waterline) varied between 34 and 39 feet (10.36–11.88 metres) during her working life; at present it is 34 feet.

6 ■ How thick is the ship's hull?

Queen Mary's hull was built using plates of best quality steel up to 30 feet (9 metres) in length, and weighing up to 3 tons each. The thickness of the hull varies between 1¼ and 2½ inches (3 and 6.5 cm) with extra reinforcement in vulnerable areas.

Queen Mary enters the King George V drydock, which was built specially for the new liner in Southampton.

The famous Cunard livery of black hull, white superstructure and black-topped 'Cunard red' funnels is applied before the new ship embarks on sea trials.

7 ■ How big are the ship's funnels?

Queen Mary's funnels, which are elliptical in shape, are not identical in size, but become progressively shorter from fore to aft. On the vessel as originally built, the forward funnel had a height of 70½ feet (21.5 metres), the middle a height of 67½ feet (20.5 metres) and aft 62¼ feet (19 metres). Each had a width of 23⅓ feet (7 metres).

8 ■ Were all three funnels functional?

During the early part of the 20th century, when shipping companies were competing for supremacy, dummy funnels or 'smoke stacks' were sometimes added to a vessel. The practice had little to do with aesthetics, but plenty to do with marketing. The travelling public understandably, yet incorrectly, associated a ship's power and capability with the number of funnels it seemed to require. To use a famous example, the public perception of *Titanic* (1912) derived partly from the ship having four funnels, although in reality the fourth was a dummy. In *Queen Mary*'s case all three funnels were functional, with large shafts running through the ship down to the engine room. Cunard must have considered her impressive enough without resorting to gimmickry.

One of the liner's vast riveted funnels is installed by a team of abseiling fitters. They were later changed during the Long Beach conversion (see question 88).

9 ■ How many lifeboats were there?

Unlike lifeboats fitted on previous ships, those on *Queen Mary* were all motorised. She had 24 boats in total: twenty were 36 feet (11 metres) long, and four were 30 feet (9 metres). Built by Hugh McLean and Sons of Goven, near Glasgow, they were collectively able to carry 3,266 people, more than her total crew and full complement of passengers, and could be launched single-handedly in less than a minute.

The ship's third siren was removed during her conversion at Long Beach and now features on *Queen Mary 2*.

10 ■ How were all the electrical items powered?

The ship was fitted with seven turbo-generators, which collectively produced up to 10,000 kilowatts of electricity. This was used to operate all kinds of equipment throughout the liner, from 30,000 light bulbs and 596 ship's clocks to projection equipment and 22 lifts (elevators). Around 4,000 miles of wiring was used throughout the vessel.

11 ■ How many sirens were there?

Queen Mary had three sirens: two on the forward funnel; one on the middle funnel. They could be heard up to 10 miles

One of the switchboards that controlled electricity for *Queen Mary's* heating and lighting, recorded in 1936.

Each of the 24 lifeboats was motorised and could be launched in less than a minute.

Workers swarm under *Queen Mary*'s giant propellers while the ship is in drydock at Southampton.

away and were known affectionately as 'The voice of *Queen Mary*'. Each siren is 6½ feet (2 metres) in length and weighs one ton. Originally they were operated by steam at a pressure of 140 psi and were tuned to 'A' (two octaves below the middle A of a piano). In her current configuration they are operated by compressed air. The pair mounted on the forward funnel still boom across the harbour daily. The third siren remained on board as part of a display until 2003 and is now installed on *Queen Mary 2* (2004), as a tribute to the grand old liner.

12 ■ What was the ship's stopping distance?

It used to take approximately 10 miles to come to a complete standstill from a cruising speed of 28.5 knots.

13 ■ Why is 'Liverpool' annotated on the stern of *Queen Mary* when her homeport was Southampton?

The place written on the stern under a vessel's name refers to her port of registration. Although Southampton was *Queen Mary*'s homeport throughout her ocean-going days, Cunard Line's main office during the 1930s was in Liverpool, which became the ship's port of registration. Cunard later moved offices to Southampton in 1965.

14 ■ What does the prefix RMS mean?

RMS refers to her fleet designation as a Royal Mail Ship. In 1839 the British Admiralty placed an advertisement for shipping companies that could transport mail between Britain and Halifax, Canada. Samuel Cunard responded and was awarded the contract for a regular transatlantic mail service, which began in May 1840. This long-term commitment acted as the catalyst for Samuel Cunard to develop his famous shipping line. The original contract was for 10 years, with Cunard receiving £55,000 per annum in quarterly payments. Nearly 100 years later *Queen Mary* was designed as the latest in a long line of Cunard ships to carry mail and the designation RMS.

Job number 534 towers over Clydebank: the world's second largest ship begins to take shape.

Building and Launch

15 ▓ Who built Britain's first 'superliner'?

The new Cunard Line ship was constructed by John Brown & Company at their famous yard on the Clyde near Glasgow, in Scotland. Brown's had a long association with Cunard, having previously built *Lusitania* (1907) and *Aquitania* (1914) for the company. The yard was initially employed to develop a design from rough sketches provided by Cunard Line, and to act as consultant to the project. Some 8,000 tank experiments were made using scale models with a length of more than 16 feet (5 metres) and eventually a blueprint was produced for the new 3-funnelled superliner. The John Brown yard was invited to tender their bid for construction along with other contenders. They were successful and in December 1930 were awarded the contract. Later that month the keel was laid for job number 534, as the project was known, and building began.

16 ▓ How much did it cost to build *Queen Mary*?

The original building costs amounted to around £5 million. This is a mere UK weekly lottery prize today, but in the early 1930s the average weekly wage for British craftsmen was three pounds and ten shillings (£3.50/$6.00), so the figure is equivalent to over £200 million ($370 million) in present terms.

17 ▓ Why did the ship take more than five years to build?

After the yard manager, Donald Skifflington, ceremoniously hammered home the very first rivet the day after Boxing Day 1930, work pressed on at

23 February 1931: construction is well under way, but work has yet to begin on the bow.

The ship's hull and superstructure were made up of plates riveted into position. Some weighed up to 3 tons and were 30 feet (9 metres) in length.

Thrust shafts prior to rough machining.

rapid speed. Britain had never seen a ship the size of 534. As the rib-like structure of the hull took shape, steel plates were riveted in place and the 12 decks laid, the giant hull dwarfed Clydebank. But the grip of the Great Depression was tightening. Cunard were able to continue trading in spite of the disastrous economy, but they weren't able to continue building 534. In early 1932, just months before the hull would have been ready for launch, work stopped. The half-completed ship then lay on her stocks for well over two years. Eventually a solution was found. Cunard was to be loaned £9.5 million pounds by the British government to finance the completion of 534 and her sistership. Work resumed in April 1934, and it was to become the first step in Britain's economic recovery. As news of the continuation of work was released, so share prices in London's stock exchange rose sharply. Six months later the new ship was ready to be launched.

18 ■ How did Cunard and White Star become one company?

As part of the loan agreement for completing 534, the British government insisted Cunard Line take over the ailing shipping company White Star Line.

One of the four 100-ton turbines produced for *Queen Mary* by John Brown & Company at Clydebank.

Workers assemble high-pressure air slots on the starboard bridge wing.

Launch day approaches: most of the supporting scaffolding has been removed and the upper hull painted in primer.

The rib-like structure of 534's hull dwarfs everything around it.

One of the ship's
20-foot (6-metre)
manganese-bronze
propellers receives a
few final touches.

White Star had once been a formidable competitor, but the company had suffered a devastating blow when their flagship liner *Titanic* sank in 1912 with the loss of 1,503 lives. The takeover was the birth of Cunard White Star.

19 ■ How many people were involved in the construction of 534?

Approximately 3,800 people worked directly on the building of the ship, many of them local men from the Clydebank area. A further 10,000 people from all round Britain, and in some cases overseas, produced thousands of components, such as parts of the stern frame and outer shaft brackets, which were cast at Darlington in the north of England. The brackets comprised eight castings that collectively weighed over 500 tons, making them the largest structural steel castings ever made. Transporting them to Clydebank was fraught with difficulty. The load was nearly the width of three train tracks and caused the temporary closure of an entire railway. At the other end of the country, 600 clocks of every description were being made at St Albans for installation throughout the ship. Still further afield, exotic woods to make colourful veneers were imported from countries of the British Empire. Job number 534 gave direct and indirect employment to thousands of people around the world.

20 ■ How big were the propellers and who made them?

The ship's original set of four propellers each had a diameter of 20 feet (6 metres) and weighed 35 tons. They were produced by the Manganese Bronze & Brass Company at a cost of £28,000. When cast they took 14 days to cool.

21 ■ How many rivets were used in constructing 534?

Ten million!

22 ■ How did Cunard decide on the name 'Queen Mary'?

Prior to the naming of 534 Cunard ships traditionally were given names ending in a distinct 'ia' sound, like *Aquitania, Mauretania* and *Berengaria*. There are several plausible stories that account for the deviation when it came to the company's new superliner. The most enduring suggests that it was no more than a misunderstanding. Cunard had intended to maintain the tradition and call their new liner 'Victoria'. A small delegation from the Line, headed by Sir Ashley Sparks, was granted an audience with King George V to seek his official approval. Sir Ashley began by stating: 'Cunard would like to name

A young rivet heater is kept busy. He and his colleagues prepared millions of steel rivets during the construction of 534.

the new ship after England's greatest queen....' Queen Mary allegedly smiled and replied: 'I would be delighted'.

23 ■ When was the ship launched?

On Wednesday, 26 September 1934, Her Majesty Queen Mary launched her namesake into the Clyde in Scotland. Millions of delighted Britons huddled round their radios listening to a live broadcast of the launch by the BBC; this was the first time that such an event had been broadcast to the entire nation.

26 September 1934: Britain's largest liner is minutes away from being launched.

At the fitting-out berth and yet to receive the Cunard colours, *Queen Mary*'s steelwork, with its ten million rivets, is highlighted by the sunlight.

HM Queen Mary launches her namesake after a bottle of Australian wine is smashed across the liner's bow.

The slipway was greased with 150 tons of tallow and 50 tons of hard soap to ensure a smooth launch.

Drag chains take-up the slack and bring the massive hull to a halt, within 2 feet (60 cm) of the calculated position.

With masts and first funnel in place *Queen Mary* begins to have a more familiar appearance.

It was also the first time that the consort of a reigning British monarch had carried out a duty of this nature. In Scotland the weather was uninviting: cold with driving rain. But despite this, large stands constructed by the shipyard were crowded with eager onlookers, who had each paid 15 shillings (75 pence) for their seat. Thousands of other people congregated on the nearby riverbanks to watch the historic event unfold, and the royal party and dignitaries gathered in a glass enclosure. After a ceremony lasting 15 minutes RMS *Queen Mary* took to the water for the first time.

24 ■ Was a bottle of Champagne broken over the ship's bow during the naming?

Champagne would probably not have been the best choice of liquid to name the new ship, as her archrival was *Normandie* of France. In the event a bottle of Australian wine was used for the christening.

25 ■ Did RMS *Queen Mary*'s size make launching difficult?

The launch was set in motion using two buttons pressed by Queen Mary. The first released equipment that held the hull back, the second activated six hydraulic rams that edged the ship into the Clyde. The slipway had been greased with tallow and soap so the launch would go smoothly. However, as the Clyde is a relatively narrow channel and the launch was only made possible after a great deal of dredging, keeping the waterborne hull from crashing into the opposite bank required very precise calculation. Drag chain weighing 2,350 tons was used to bring the vessel to a halt. The mathematics behind this were the responsibility of a young man named John Brown, who was later involved in the design of both *Queen Elizabeth* and *Queen Elizabeth 2*.

26 ■ What happened after the launch?

Inside the great steel hull, fitters and craftsmen install thousands of components supplied from all over Britain and the Commonwealth.

At the point of launching, *Queen Mary* was little more than a vast steel shell. Within an hour of touching the water the hull was towed to a nearby fitting-out berth so the next phase of building could begin. Twenty-four watertube boilers and the massive engines and machinery were installed, her masts set, and three giant funnels craned into place. Some 4,000 miles of wiring were laid; safety equipment including 66 watertight doors was fitted; and the ship's vast kitchens constructed. Next came the furniture and finishes that set new standards in opulence at sea. Craftspeople from every conceivable trade toiled side by side for the following 18 months to complete the grand masterpiece.

Within 18 months of her launch *Queen Mary* was transformed from empty shell to luxury liner.

Navigating the relatively narrow River Clyde was a potentially hazardous journey, which required careful calculation.

Wood panelling is painstakingly installed. Much of the panelling in First Class remains to this day but was modernised with a covering of leather during the post-war refit.

27 ■ How did Cunard publicise their new ship?

Due to the significance of the project, the press were very willing to cover the story. The ghostly image of the half-finished hull languishing on the stocks became synonymous with the Great Depression and consequently triumphant images of the eventual return to work were also published with enthusiasm. It was a good story and people from all walks of life were eager to read the next instalment. But the corporate publicity machine was also working to ensure interest was maintained. A fascinating set of comparisons was worked out as a way to convey the sheer size of the liner. In reference to the length of the funnel shaft from boiler room to top of fore funnel (a length of 184 feet [56 metres]): 'If one of *Queen Mary*'s funnels were set upon its side, three full-size British express locomotives could pass through it abreast, alternatively, if it were set still on its side, in Trafalgar Square, the upper rim would be level with the roof of the portico of the National Gallery. In length too these mighty cylinders are breathtaking… equal to the height of Big Ben.' The statistics and drawings that accompanied the comparisons were very successful. Alongside their appearance in numerous contemporary newspapers and magazines of 1936, they also featured in a book published to commemorate the ship's maiden voyage.

Nearly seventy years later a similar book was produced to celebrate Cunard's new cruise ship, the first liner of the 21st century, *Queen Mary 2*. References are made to the first *Queen Mary* and statistics concerning the new vessel are presented in a similar manner to those in the 1930s: 'Four of the mighty Eurostar locomotives that speed through the Channel Tunnel would fit into *Queen Mary 2*'s funnel, 44 feet by 22 feet [13.5 by 6.7 metres] at its widest point.' Of course, the new ship has only one funnel…

Queen Mary was big news: a variety of special publications marked her inception.

The First Class Restaurant on C Deck never fails to impress. Large enough to accommodate all First Class passengers at once, it was one of the largest rooms created on board a vessel.

Design and Technology

28 ■ What style or theme did her interiors follow?

As a product of the early 1930s *Queen Mary*'s interior styling is predominantly Art Deco, with a hint of Art Nouveau. Cunard were keen to establish their new ship as a credible rival to the French superliner *Normandie*. In reality the French offering was a stylised, extravagant showcase of French artistry subsidised by government money. The British vessel was to be warmer and less fussy, yet still exude grandeur and luxury. The interiors were designed by Arthur J. Davis and Benjamin W. Morris. Their First Class Restaurant was one of the largest rooms afloat: 143 feet (43.3 metres) long, 118 feet (35.5 metres) wide, the full width of the ship, and up to 27 feet (8.3 metres) high. The proportions alone are impressive; the overall effect was further enhanced with extensive use of natural woods, artwork and 1930s detailing.

Other areas of the ship, such as the First Class Swimming Pool, are pure Art Deco. The pool features uncluttered, clear-cut lines. The walls were orig-

inally covered in handmade 'faience' tiles the colour of straw, with bands in emerald green and bright red. Chunky columns add weight and grandeur to the room and contrast with a mother of pearl ceiling. The uplighters, signs and bold double staircase leading to the viewing gallery are highly evocative of the 1930s. In other parts of the ship the theme is continued. First Class stairways feature unexpected treats such as glass panels etched with images of 1930s transport, and staterooms contain a wealth of Art Deco influence, including characteristic bathroom fittings. In Second and Third the

The Second Class Bar has long been removed, but was originally located on Main Deck.

A. R. Thomson's 'Royal Jubilee Week 1935' features in the First Class Observation Lounge.

The First Class Starboard Gallery was often used with the adjoining Ballroom.

theme of wood panelling and warm colours was maintained. Public rooms in Third were comfortable, and Second Class quite luxurious, but less grand, due largely to much lower ceilings. Geometric patterns on carpet and fabrics, and Mackintosh-style light shades once again highlight fashions of the day.

29 ■ Was the artwork on board specially commissioned?

An army of artists was commissioned to produce sculptures, carvings, friezes and paintings, which have become famous features of *Queen Mary*. Among the best known is Doris Zinkeisen's mural for the Verandah Grill, which was an exclusive restaurant enjoyed by First Class passengers, who had to pay £1.00 per head for the privilege. Effectively, Zinkeisen's paintings were the only decoration, as unlike other areas there was no panelling. The themes were originally theatre, pantomime and circus, with the addition of film when the artist restored her work during the post-war refit.

In contrast to the nightclub atmosphere of the Grill, the First Class Smoking Room had all the hallmarks of a traditional gentleman's club, including dark wood panels and decorative carvings. Artist Edward Wadsworth was commissioned to produce two large paintings with a maritime theme. 'The Sea' has a surrealistic feel, and features images of large shells. Closer study reveals *Queen Mary* steaming into the picture from the horizon. 'Dressed Overall at the Quay' is over 10 feet (3 metres) high and includes a clever optical illusion: from any angle the viewer seems to look down a plank painted in the foreground.

The First Class Restaurant has work from many different artists: Walter and Donald Gilbert produced ornate bronze doors depicting Castor and Pollux, the guardians of sailors.

More than thirty prominent artists of the day were commissioned to produce original artwork for the ship.

Edward Wadsworth completes 'Dressed Overall at the Quay', still a focal point of the First Class Smoking Room.

MacDonald Gill's famous decorative map of the North Atlantic Ocean, a feature of the First Class Restaurant.

A series of carvings by Bainbridge Copnall illustrates the history of ship-building, and Duncan Carse was commissioned to produce painted panels featuring birds from each side of the Atlantic. By far the largest single artwork was the decorative map of the North Atlantic by MacDonald Gill. Two tracks representing summer and winter routes of *Queen Mary* carried a crystal model of the ship, which was moved each day of a voyage to mark her progress. Like Doris Zinkeisen, MacDonald Gill took the opportunity to update his work after the Second World War, when he added the new RMS *Queen Elizabeth* to the New York side of the map.

For many First Class passengers, 'Royal Jubilee Week 1935' by A. R. Thomson was a firm favourite. Located above the bar in the Observation Lounge, the large oil conveys all the colour and merriment of the historic occasion. It was a topical subject when *Queen Mary* entered service and decades later the painting has lost none of its charm.

30 ▦ Is it true one room featured an open fire?

As unlikely as it seems, there was a real coal-burning fire on board. This was something of a legacy from liners of the past that reflected all the trappings and comforts of life at home, however impractical or dangerous. In *Queen Mary*'s case the working fireplace was located in the very traditional First Class Smoking Room. It ceased to be used after the Second World War.

31 ■ Was the ship technically advanced for her time?

Externally *Queen Mary* was pretty traditional even in the 1930s. Even her engines and boilers were of tried and tested design. But there were some very innovative features. Fire safety was a big issue and a comprehensive system was installed. It not only pinpointed an area of danger, but allowed officers to seal sections of the ship and action extinguishers remotely from a central fire station. Independently controlled sprinklers were the main type of extinguisher, but below decks in the area where passengers' cars were garaged, there was a very sophisticated carbon-dioxide gas system. In the kitchens, up-to-date technology was also put to good use: original labour-saving equipment included electric potato-peeling machines and dishwashers.

32 ■ What were the most novel features of *Queen Mary*?

One item to gain special mention was the wireless equipment. Broadcast radio programmes could be received and redistributed around the ship, through an advanced system featuring 38 loudspeakers in various locations. As one commentator put it: '…when we are dancing to Henry Hall in England, hundreds and hundreds at sea in the *Queen Mary* may be doing

An image of 1930s elegance: the luxurious First Class Lounge.

The indoor Second Class Swimming Pool was a first for any liner.

the same.' The system also allowed passengers to listen to events held in another part of the ship: a performance by the Orchestra in the Main Lounge, for example, might be relayed to the Second Class Lounge and one of the Third Class public rooms; dance music played in the Ball Room might be piped to passengers in the Verandah Grill.

Another ingenious feature of the ship was the 'Thyratron-Reactor Lighting Control', installed in the First Class Main Lounge and Verandah Grill. This device allowed music and lighting to be played as one. The tone and intensity of music would be processed by the system and sets of red, green and blue lights were activated by a signal. It could be operated by a solo instrument or full orchestra and allowed the music to automatically change the lighting effect of the room. It was a remarkable piece of 1930s technology.

A further, rather eccentric, item also came under the general heading of lighting: the ship's kennels were situated forward of the second funnel, port side of the Sports Deck. When King Edward (later Duke of Windsor) visited the ship at Clydebank he was shown the kennels. His Majesty joked at a lack of any lampposts for the dogs to use, and soon after one was installed. It remained a feature of the ship until 1967 when it was transferred to *Queen Elizabeth 2*.

33 ■ How did *Queen Mary* differ from her contemporaries?

In relation to most ships already in service, *Queen Mary* was progressive. She took levels of comfort across the classes to new heights, and offered unique features such as an indoor swimming pool in Second Class. And of course she was larger and faster than any previous ship, except the flagship of French Line. *Queen Mary* was a new breed; in a time before longhaul flights were anticipated, it was expected that ocean liners would continue to grow in size and capacity. The only real comparisons to be made are with *Normandie* and *Queen Elizabeth*. Each was fundamentally similar, yet quite distinct. Being French, *Normandie* (1935) exuded chic design and overwhelming luxury. She was very modern, with clean cut, uncluttered lines. Even essential items like ventilation shafts were stylized and hidden as part of the modern design. She was also technically advanced, featuring a state-of-the-art propulsion system. The two-funnelled *Queen Elizabeth* bore much greater similarity to *Queen Mary*, although she too was slightly more streamline. Her overall concept was more an evolution in design than direct copy, which provided the sisters with a level of individuality.

34 ■ Was there a Crow's Nest?

Queen Mary has a Crow's Nest, which was manned by a lookout. Like many of the liner's features, it set a new standard. Located just over halfway up the foremast, 130 feet (40 metres) above the sea, *Queen Mary*'s Crow's Nest was positively luxurious compared with many. Accessed by 110 steps inside the mast, via a door on B deck, it has a roof and weather screen, and during the

Queen Mary's Crow's Nest, halfway up the foremast, offered commanding views (on this occasion over her yard at Clydebank).

ship's sea-going days was provided with a telephone link to the Bridge and an electric heater to stave off the chill of a North Atlantic winter.

35 ■ Has the ship been altered much since her launch?

Throughout their working lives liners receive regular refits and public areas are often subject to change. *Queen Mary* is no exception. The most striking alterations were made during the post-war refit when the liner was restored to passenger ship from troop-carrier. At this time a number of public areas were completely remodelled. However, the main alterations came in the late 1960s, after the ship was taken out of service. There have been many changes, but enough originality is retained to get a real sense of the past. Externally, *Queen Mary* appears virtually as she was during her Atlantic-crossing days.

36 ■ Has the ship's design had any influence on the new *Queen Mary 2*?

Queen Mary was a major influence when the design team responsible for the interior of the new ship looked back at liners of the past. They visited the ship in Long Beach and carried out detailed research. But a conscious decision was made not to simply replicate the first 'QM'. Says designer Andy Collier:

Changes in fabric and carpet pattern reveal this as a post-war view of the First Class Lounge.

The Second Class Restaurant (left) is less grand than that in First Class. The First Class Drawing Room (right) served also as the Catholic Chapel. When not in use the altar was concealed behind the folding screen, which featured a painting by Kenneth Shoesmith.

'We wanted to 'cherry-pick' ideas and then update them with a more contemporary feel.' There are details and elements of the original *Queen Mary* waiting to be discovered by those who recognise them. They subtly invoke the atmosphere of the so-called 'golden age of travel' and bring an innovative freshness to well-loved tradition. The forward-facing Commodore Club reflects the feel of the old ship's Observation Lounge, with its sweeping curves and raised levels at each side, but a modern twist is achieved through the use of new colours and patterns. The famous decorative map by MacDonald Gill designed for *Queen Mary*'s First Class Restaurant (see question 29) is echoed in a piece commissioned for the Atrium aboard *QM2*. And there are various other discreet influences from the past, including the design of decorative banding and light fittings.

When *Queen Mary* embarked upon her maiden voyage in 1936 she was the largest and fastest ship ever built by Britain. At her inception in 2004, *Queen Mary 2*, like her namesake, went straight into the record books as the largest liner the world had ever seen. The two great vessels have a great deal more in common than simply a name.

Capstans and winch gear at the forward end of Main Deck were all electrically operated.

Crew and Passengers

37 ■ How many passengers were carried?

Queen Mary was an ocean liner rather than a cruise ship; her role was to carry passengers on a regular service route. Three classes of accommodation were offered. Their designations were changed during the post-Second World War refit (see question 50). First (originally Cabin) Class was the most lavish and expensive, and was situated in the central, most comfortable part of the ship where there was least movement. It could accommodate 776 people in pampered luxury. Up to 784 could be carried in Second Class, which was aft of the ship. This class was originally known as Tourist Class, but was renamed Cabin (the old First Class designation) in the post-war era. Decor and fittings were less lavish, but a high level of comfort remained. With the ship's engines located below, however, there was some vibration. The least desirable

Queen Mary's Second Steward Joe Rigby inspects a group of bell boys on a post-war crossing.

Passengers' luggage would be labelled to show if it were 'wanted on voyage' and either taken to staterooms or carried in the hold.

Southampton florists deliver bouquets to staterooms; it was a stylish way for family and friends to wish passengers 'bon voyage'.

The Duke and Duchess of Windsor were among *Queen Mary*'s many regulars.

passenger accommodation was Third (later Tourist) Class, at the forward end of the vessel. This could hold 579 people, who had to endure violent pitching on rough winter passages as the liner battled the rigours of the Atlantic. Many people travelling Third would have been European emigrants starting new lives in the United States or Canada. The classes were strictly segregated, with gates across corridors preventing intermixing and their own gangways for embarking and disembarking.

Queen Mary was designed to carry a complement of 2,139 passengers across the classes and a crew of 1,101, but during the years of the Second World War that all changed (see question 68). By the end of her ocean-going days *Queen Mary* had carried nearly three million passengers.

38 ▧ How much luggage would passengers have taken?

Passengers were expected to have a reasonable volume of luggage, particularly if they were touring the United States. The journey itself often required quite a wardrobe for ladies, who dressed for dinner and were never seen in the same gown twice. Many people managed with a trunk and perhaps one or two additional items, but one society couple regularly travelled with 80 suitcases in their suite and another 75 in the ship's hold.

39 ▧ Did stewards really 'go to any lengths' to help passengers?

Cunard earned an enviable reputation for excellent service. Restaurant comment books reveal that on the very rare occasions when passengers were dissatisfied, the Restaurant Manager would often visit them in their stateroom and personally order special dishes. Waiters and the chef would also be informed so the passenger received individual attention.

Stewards endeavoured to accommodate the passengers' every whim (see question 42). Regular visitors the Duke and Duchess of Windsor always stayed in Suite 58 on Main Deck. It was relatively modest, comprising three rooms. As privileged passengers the Windsors could make special requests, and so the Duchess used to send advance details of her desired colour scheme. It was usually electric blues and greens. On one voyage she mentioned her dislike of the furniture... it was dutifully changed, mid-Atlantic!

40 ▧ How long were waiters on duty each day?

Waiters worked very long hours. Breakfast was served from 7:30 am, but the work continued until 10:30 am. After a short break waiting staff would be on

With up to 40,000 meals to prepare each voyage, there was almost constant activity in the kitchens.

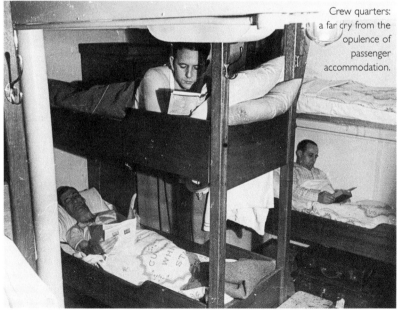

Crew quarters: a far cry from the opulence of passenger accommodation.

duty again serving lunch. Lunch would be cleared by 2:30 pm providing the chance for another break for an hour or two before afternoon tea. An hour-and-a-half later, wearing evening uniform, waiters would be back at their stations preparing for dinner, which was served at 7:30 pm. In First Class all passengers dined at a single sitting. This became a social highlight and would often last several unhurried hours; some waiters even slipped to the crew bar for a pint in between courses It was an exhausting routine. Waiters were very rarely able to manage six hours' sleep, before starting all over again.

41 ■ Could telephone calls be made at sea?

One of many supplements about the ship published in 1936 made special mention of the liner's communication links: 'The telephony system is so wonderful that passengers in the ship, even when she is far out in the Atlantic, can ring up anyone in the world, and do it without the possibility of confi-

Queen Mary's stock of linen comprised 500,000 items. This was in fact a triplicate stock. One set was held on the ship, with the others at New York and Southampton for a quick turn-around.

dential conversation being over-heard.'In the early days this was yet another example of cutting-edge technology. On one occasion a businessman urgently needed to contact a colleague whom he knew to be travelling cross-country by train. He telephoned the rail company with a message, which was relayed down the line and delivered to the man in person by a Station Master.

A post-war view of the telephone kiosks, which were located in the First Class Prom Deck Square.

42 ■ Were crew given tips?

Tipping was very much a part of life aboard the liners. It was a practice that filtered down from passengers as a means of keeping the wheels of good service well-oiled. At the sharp

The telephone exchange aboard *Queen Mary* was as large as many on land. First Class staterooms were each provided with a 'phone enabling communication around the ship and ashore.

end stewards took a pride in their work. They remembered personal likes and dislikes of regular passengers and tried to anticipate their needs This not only upheld the good name of the ship and company, but often led to a decent tip at the end of the voyage. To make sure a steward or stewardess could deliver their passengers' requests, they would pass a tip to pantrymen, who in turn tipped their chef to secure priority service. It was an unofficial, yet very efficient system that appeased everyone. Other members of crew, such as lift boys and bell boys, were not necessarily reliant on other people to provide a good service, although

At your service! For lads in their mid teens position of bell boy aboard *Queen Mary* was highly sought after.

their roles often offered less opportunity to attract a significant gratuity. One baby-faced young man stumbled on an effective method of increasing his income. The youngster was assigned to door duty. He gave an engaging grin to each passenger as he opened the door for them. One man remarked on his broad smile and the lad immediately responded with: 'Thank you sir, it's my birthday.' The gentleman wished him many happy returns and gave him a tip for his trouble. Every day for the following weeks it was the boy's birthday! He was eventually rumbled and ordered to stop his little ruse.

43 ■ What was the 'golden rivet'?

Allegedly, in the days before steel plates were welded together, a pure gold rivet was randomly used somewhere in a ship's construction. The myth was propagated by old 'sea dogs', who regaled naive young crew members with the tale. There are many lads in the *Queen Mary* crew who remember scraping the paint off rivet heads below deck in the hope they would discover her elusive 'golden rivet'. What they would have done had they found it is anyone's guess.

The First Class Library (above) located at the forward end of Promenade Deck (port side), carried up to 1,700 books. The Second Class Gymnasium (below), was for more active pursuits.

Life Aboard

44 ■ When was *Queen Mary*'s maiden voyage?

Cunard Line was inundated with requests for tickets for the ship's inaugural crossing. Two thousand places were available, but ten times that number could have been sold. Fares during the ship's first season ranged from £18 and 10 shillings for a single Third Class passage, to £102 for a First Class return.

On 27 May 1936 *Queen Mary* left Southampton on her maiden voyage. It was an event that attracted media attention from around the world. One hundred of the passengers were reporters eager to record every detail for their readers, and presenters from the BBC broadcast live while at sea. As the ship made her way down Southampton Water tens of thousands of cheering

RMS *Queen Mary*'s maiden voyage from Southampton took place on 27 May 1936.

people lined the shores. It was a voyage that would prove memorable for many reasons. The first port of call was Cherbourg for the embarkation of further passengers. New facilities had been built by the French specifically for *Queen Mary*, but due to an unfortunate error the retractable gangway proved 6 feet (1.8 metres) too short. After two hours a makeshift extension was constructed and the ship continued on her way to New York.

As well as fare-paying passengers and reporters, two stowaways managed to sneak aboard. One of them was discovered early in the voyage and put ashore at Cherbourg, but the other, Frank Gardner, an unemployed labourer, wasn't detected until later, and so worked his passage in the kitchens.

Many people hoped *Queen Mary* would make a record-breaking crossing. It looked likely until fog during the latter stage of the crossing slowed the ship, making her average speed a respectable 29.13 knots. The arrival in New York on 1 June was suitably spectacular. Thousands of Americans took the day off work in order to witness her loud and colourful entrance, and hundreds of small craft escorted the liner up the Hudson River to her new berth at Pier 90. One passenger later wrote to Cunard: '...there were no doubts in the minds of the enthusiastic passengers on board that she will reign as Queen of the Seas for many years to come'.

The ship receives a spectacular welcome on her maiden arrival in New York, 1 June 1936.

45 ■ How did *Queen Mary* win the Blue Riband?

Queen Mary held the Blue Riband trophy for 14 years.

The Blue Riband trophy was awarded for the fastest round trip across the Atlantic Ocean by liner. Cunard made a statement claiming they were in no mood for racing. This reassuringly cautious approach was in part a legacy of the *Titanic* disaster earlier in the century, but in private who could deny the kudos of the title 'fastest ship in the world'? During the ship's first season in 1936 a record-breaking round trip was made, and the Blue Riband taken from rival liner *Normandie* (1935) of the French Line. The new record was 4 days, 4 hours and 12 minutes eastbound, and 4 days, 6 hours and 20 minutes westbound. *Normandie* raised the stakes with a successful challenge, but *Queen Mary* responded with an even faster time in 1938. On 8 August a new record of 3 days, 21 hours and 48 minutes eastbound was set – 1 hour 14 minutes faster than *Normandie*. This time the British liner retained the record for 14 years until it was smashed by the revolutionary new SS *United States* in 1952. Cunard's *Queen Elizabeth* (1940) never laid claim to the Blue Riband. She might well have been able to break the record set by her sister, but their operator was happy to publicise the post-war transatlantic duo as the largest and fastest ships in the world.

46 ■ Could passengers expect a smooth crossing on such a large vessel?

Most first-time passengers may have expected a smooth crossing, but if they travelled in winter months they would experience something quite different. A severe and unexpected rolling action became apparent in October 1936 as the ship encountered bad weather. This was so unexpected that designers had not included handrails for public passageways in the original specification, and furniture wasn't secured to decks as it was in many other liners. During the first 'rough' crossing alone 12 people sustained injury, and a number of ambulances were called to meet the ship at Southampton. It was so serious a problem that questions were raised in parliament on how Cunard Line intended to improve passenger safety and comfort.

A team of carpenters travelled with the ship to install the vital handrails. Heavy items of furniture were bolted down and a number of chairs were kept in place using

One of *Queen Mary*'s stabilizer fins is inspected in drydock, March 1958.

detachable leashes. In the restaurants waiters did their best to prevent the tableware slipping around, but more than 25,000 items of china and glass continued to be broken each year. The rolling itself wasn't cured for over twenty years and remained a 'characteristic' until stabilizers were fitted in 1958.

47 ■ Did she suffer any other initial problems?

There were one or two teething difficulties that needed attention, including smuts from the funnels on the open decks and, much more serious, severe vibration at the stern. The latter was a great embarrassment for *Queen Mary*'s operator. It was also very costly to put right. In December 1936, at the end of the first season, the ship was drydocked in Southampton for a fortnight to undergo major alterations. Lounges were stripped and rebuilt with extra structural stiffening. The ship's four propellers were replaced. And modifications were made to overcome the problem of smoke smuts. In March 1937 Captain Peel, *Queen Mary*'s new Master, reported the vibration had been 'practically eliminated' by the revisions.

48 ■ What sort of people travelled on liners like *Queen Mary*?

In an age when there was no option but to travel by ocean liner if going overseas, ships like *Queen Mary* carried people from all walks of life and of various nationalities. Although the glamour of life aboard such ships has captured public imagination, at the opposite end of the scale thousands of ordinary people travelled Third Class. Many were from across Europe and would join *Queen Mary* at Cherbourg in France. At a time when it was very rare for the working classes to take a holiday abroad, many Third Class passengers would be travelling on business or emigrating to the New World. Second Class would have appealed to the British middle class who enjoyed a good standard of living at home and could afford more than a basic passage.

In the pre-war First Class, captains of industry, stars of stage and silver screen, royalty and politicians rubbed shoulders. *Queen Mary* was fashionable and held in high esteem, so naturally attracted prominent figures of the day. It was an aspect of travel which eluded many ships and one that wouldn't be carried-over to travel by air in future years, with the exception of Concorde.

49 ■ How did the Class System work?

The ship was divided into three classes, which varied in opulence, decorative detail and proportion (see question 37). Their original designations of Cabin, Tourist and Third were changed after the war (see question 50). But the class system was more than simply grades of accommodation. In many ways it reflected the structure of society in Britain; a society that relied on people knowing their place. Aboard *Queen Mary* and her like, the various classes were segregated. Locked or manned gates prevented passengers from roaming from one section to another. Each had its own entrance and amenities, and crew. Each was essentially self contained. It could be argued this was only right: why should a passenger paying a lower fare enjoy the same benefits as someone who had paid much more? But an undercurrent of social hierarchy and fear

Just a few of the celebrity passengers who travelled on board the ship: Winston Churchill, David Niven, Fred Astaire, and Laurel & Hardy.

of upsetting the status quo also played a part. Social climbing was not on the agenda. That said, *Queen Mary*'s Third Class accommodation rivalled First Class aboard some older ships in service, and quality cuisine was served throughout, limited only in choice in Third (see question 54).

50 ■ Why was Cabin Class renamed after the Second World War?

The renaming, which affected all three classes and deck names throughout the ship, was essentially to do with marketing and the ship's relaunch. When *Queen Mary* first went into service, pre-war Britain, like other western countries, was struggling through the Great Depression. The economy was bleak. Calling the least luxurious grade of accommodation Third made the class sound more affordable. This was still an important segment of the market for ship operators. But in a post-war era of hope and optimism classes aboard the liner were changed to First, Cabin and Tourist, suggesting an upgrade throughout. Decks were re-designated too. C Deck became R Deck because it was the main deck for the ship's restaurants, and all decks below were changed by one letter: D became C, E became D, through to H Deck. The name changes may sound insignificant now, but in the context of layout revisions, fresh furniture, decor and carpeting, they provided a real sense of newness.

A Second Class stateroom in 1936 was not panelled in wood like those in First Class, but was spacious and comfortable.

A First Class suite converted for use as a dining room in 1936. Twin beds could easily be installed in place of the dining suite.

51 ■ What food was on offer?

Cuisine aboard *Queen Mary* rivalled the best European hotels. The menu was rich and varied. Chefs could proudly produce anything a passenger wished for, even if it were not on the

One of Cunard White Star's best-known posters: an enduring and glamourous image evocative of the 'golden age of travel', which has since been reproduced in many forms. *(Courtesy of Marine Art Posters)*

The Roman Catholic altarpiece *Madonna of the Atlantic* by Kenneth Shoesmith is installed in the FIrst Class Drawing Room. *(Courtesy of the Madame Yevonde Portrait Archive)*

Finishing touches are made to the First Class Children's Playroom. *(Courtesy of the Madame Yevonde Portrait Archive)*

In the Second Class Lounge, workmen position an etched niche mirror, the work of artist Margot Gilbert. (*Courtesy of the Madame Yevonde Portrait Archive*)

The First Class Observation Lounge with views forward over the bow became a favourite spot for the rich and famous to congregate. (*Courtesy of the Madame Yevonde Portrait Archive*)

These period colour illustrations are the work of Madame Yevonde, a prominent 1930s society photographer. They were recorded during the latter stages of *Queen Mary*'s completion, while artists and craftsmen were at work. A few weeks later the ship was in service. The complete series comprises 15 images, which are believed to be the very first colour photographs of their type ever recorded. Images from the 3,000-strong Madame Yevonde Portrait Archive continue to feature in exhibitions around the world. See Bibliography and Sources for details.

The Second Class Playroom nears completion. The raised platform in the corner supported a train set which ran around the room. *(Courtesy of the Madame Yevonde Portrait Archive)*

The First Class Restaurant captured in an early publicity photograph. *(Eric Sauder Collection)*

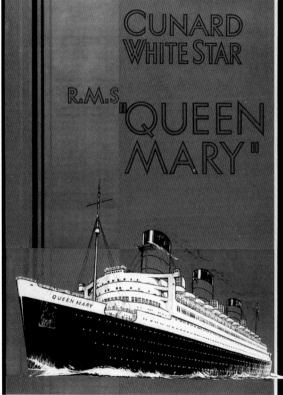

Baggage labels, menu covers and brochures from the 1930s–'60s evoke a past era, and have become extremely collectable. *(Courtesy of Marine Art Posters)*

Another iconic poster from the 1930s promising luxury travel to foreign climes. It was an elegant age for those wealthy enough to seek adventure. *(Courtesy of Marine Art Posters)*

Another publicity image issued by Cunard Line depicting luxury dining aboard *Queen Mary* in the First Class Restaurant. *(Eric Sauder Collection)*

The First Class Swimming Pool today. Virtually as it was during the ship's ocean-going days, the pool remains a wonderful example of 1930s styling, but is no longer used. *(Author)*

Queen Mary at her permanent berth in Long Beach. The rock dyke to the right allows water to pass in and out of the lagoon, and protects the ship from debris and other vessels. (Author)

Shortly after dawn: Queen Mary lies in tranquil retirement in Long Beach, California. (Author)

The First Class Restaurant today, featuring MacDonald Gill's decorative map of the North Atlantic. The area beneath was originally open; the panelling was realigned during conversion work in Long Beach (see questions 29 and 74). (Author)

Queen Mary's foredeck is much as it was before the ship went out of service, although a gangway now links this area to the rest of Main Deck across the well deck. *(Author)*

A large sitting room, which formed part of a First Class suite, in 1936. A system of interconnecting rooms offered great flexibility; when Count Rossi of Martin-Rossi travelled aboard his accommodation comprised a suite of twenty rooms.

menu. On one occasion a group of American oil tycoons put them to the test by ordering rattlesnake soup. The company's faultless reputation remained intact when the quick-thinking Chief Steward served baked eel while waiters shook baby rattles!

52 ■ How much food was consumed each trip?

The variety and quantities of provisions were vast: 4,000 gallons of milk; 70,000 eggs; 11,000 lb of fresh fish; 50,000 lb of potato; 50,000 lb of mixed vegetables; 77,000 lb of meat; 2,000 lb of cheese; 11,000 lb of

A Third Class stateroom in 1936; all had hot and cold water, the latest form of ventilation, dressing tables, individual berth lamps, and never more than four berths.

sugar; 4,000 lb of tea and coffee; and 100 lb of caviar. The ship's wine cellar carried 15,000 bottles of wine and spirits, 40,000 bottles of beer and 60,000 of mineral water. A crew of 120 kitchen staff produced 40,000 meals each crossing.

Just a proportion of the ship's provisions at Southampton waiting to be loaded in March 1939.

53 ■ When were meals served?

First Class: Breakfast 8:00 am
                  Lunch 1:00 pm
                  Dinner 7:30 pm

Verandah Grill: Lunch 12:00 pm
                  Dinner 7:00 pm

Second Class: Breakfast 8:00 am & 9:00 am
                  Lunch 12:15 pm & 1:30 pm
                  Dinner 6:30 pm & 7:45 pm

Third Class   Breakfast 7:30 am & 8:30 am
                  Lunch 12:30 pm & 1:30 pm
                  Dinner 6:30 pm & 7:30 pm

For each class morning soup was served at 11:00 am and afternoon tea at 4:00 pm.

54 ■ How much choice was there on an average menu?

First Class passengers had the widest culinary choice. Up to 18 breakfast cereals would be on offer, a choice of eight aperitifs at dinner and nine desserts, among a total of seven courses. Even Third Class, which offered least choice, was very impressive, with five aperitifs and three desserts from which to choose. Menus appeared in English except for

Chefs proudly offered to produce anything a passenger ordered, even if it were not on the menu.

Third Class, which was in English and French as a courtesy to the high proportion of European passengers emigrating to the United States.

55 ■ How were passengers entertained?

Unlike cruise ships today the old liners did not run a programme of round-the-clock organised entertainment. There was, however, plenty to keep passengers amused. First and Second Class sections of the ship each had an indoor swimming pool and gymnasium; First also had a squash court. Traditional deck games like quoits and shuffleboard were popular throughout, as was the 'daily tote' whereby passengers would place wagers on the number of miles the ship had covered in the day.

Although there was not originally a purpose-built cinema, provision was made for film shows in other areas of the ship, such as the Third Class Smoking Room and First Class

Queen Mary's Art Deco First Class Swimming Pool.

Lounge, which has a projection room hidden behind the massive gesso panel. There was a resident orchestra on board and guest entertainers made special appearances: harmonica player Larry Adler played for audiences on the maiden voyage and in the late 1950s singer Rosemary Squires performed a series of concerts that were broadcast from mid-Atlantic by BBC Radio. Dances were a routine fixture. During the evening the luxury Wilton carpet in the First Class Lounge was rolled back to reveal a parquet dance floor. The orchestra would play on until the very last couple left the floor, even sometimes playing though the night.

56 ■ Were there areas of the ship that catered for children?

Each level of accommodation had its own playroom. First Class was lavish and featured extra touches like a built-in slide, sentry box, log hut and three 'caves' beneath the slide. And there was a cinema area where children could watch cartoons; projection equipment was operated by a button that the children could press. Second Class included a large model railway which ran

A view of the First Class Playroom. Alongside the usual toys and games, the room originally also featured a small aquarium.

three sides of the room and an aeroplane that 'flew' along a wire. The Third Class equivalent was relatively austere. It featured plenty of toys and games, but looked more classroom than playroom. None of the rooms survive in their original form today.

57 ■ What services were available to passengers?

Ships such as *Queen Mary* were virtually floating villages. Each class offered a wide range of services and amenities, which varied in scale. The First Class Shopping Centre on Promenade Deck was the most spacious and elaborate. It included three stores: W. H. Smith & Son, which sold books and magazines, clothing retailer Austin Reed of London, and The Promenade Shop, which sold tobacco and souvenirs. There was also a branch of Austin Reed in Second Class, located off the Second Class entrance. Those travelling in Third could buy sundry items at the 'B Deck Shop'. Branches of Midland Bank were located throughout the liner and there was a hair salon and gentlemen's barbers for each class. Children were catered for, with a well-equipped playroom in each part of the vessel (see question 56). And there was also a dog-walking service for passengers travelling with pets. Dogs were kept in the kennels on the Sports Deck and overseen by the ship's butcher.

The First Class Promenade Shop, recorded in 1936, was privately owned. It sold a wide range of ornaments, soft toys and other gifts and souvenirs.

The First Class Austin Reed store. *Queen Mary* souvenir handkerchiefs were on sale at seven shillings and sixpence.

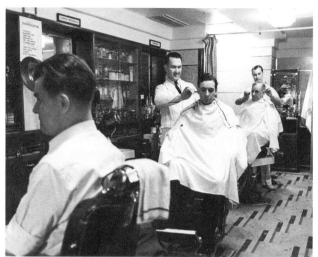

The Second Class gentlemen's barbers.

The Second Class Austin Reed store is re-stocked.

First and Second Classes each had their own well-ordered travel bureau, where passengers could obtain tourist information, book tickets and tours, and make hotel reservations all within a short walk of their cabin.

58 ■ How were passengers kept informed of events?

A public address system was installed, supplied by Marconi, but for more detailed information every cabin received a copy of the on-board newspaper, the *Ocean Times*. This was produced by the ship's own printing department, along with the daily menus and special items, including the invitations to dine at Table 199, the Captain's table. The press worked overtime during the Second World War when *Queen Mary* was working as a troop-carrier, turning out bulletins to keep soldiers up-to-date on world events. The wartime newssheets were named *The Troops Tatler* and *Ammo Daily*.

59 ■ Was *Queen Mary* self-sufficient?

Queen Mary was about as self-sufficient as an ocean liner could be. There were vast insulated storerooms designed to keep produce in prime condition,

Despite being a small department, the ship's on-board print shop was of great importance. It produced menus, programmes, a daily newspaper and other items, many of them illustrated.

plus a butchery and bakery and a number of crew who provided an extremely wide range of culinary skills. The ship had its own laundry, electrical generators and water-softening plant. A comprehensively equipped hospital was located on B Deck aft, and the ship's gardener took care of the hundreds of potted plants. As well as the usual hotel services, Cunard provided, as far as possible, everything available at home, from a Kosher Pantry to Rotary Club meetings. And the liner was unique in having Catholic and Protestant chapels and a Synagogue. *Queen Mary* was famously a happy ship. The goodwill and camaraderie amongst crew members made her a true community at sea.

60 ■ What was the ship's route?

Queen Mary's usual route was between Southampton and New York, calling both eastbound and westbound at Cherbourg. The actual course varied according to the time of year. Her winter route was slightly more southerly to avoid ice and the worst North Atlantic weather. During the Second World War the ship ventured into various other areas of the world (see question 67), and during the latter stage of her time in service *Queen Mary* cruised to places like the Canaries. Her last voyage took her around Cape Horn to the west coast of America (see questions 77 and 79).

61 ■ What was the ship's most difficult voyage?

Aside the perilous wartime voyages, one of *Queen Mary*'s most dangerous passages was her first: the short 15-mile journey down the River Clyde from the John Brown yard. The Clyde had been specially dredged and the ship kept as light as possible. Even lifeboats were left off except for two forward boats each side. At 9:45 on the morning of 24 March 1936, the ship cast-off and within minutes the bow was stuck in mud. She lay lengthways across the river. After around 30 minutes the ship was eased back and turned downriver. The journey continued slowly, with seven tugs to keep the liner in check. An hour later there was more drama. Now under her own steam *Queen Mary* went off course and swung towards the north shore, dragging the forward tugs with her. The ship was aground just 15 feet (4.5 metres) from the river bank. Excitable onlookers were able to chat with people on board before the ship was tugged back to the deep water channel and on her way again. It was an anxious moment. In the event there was no real damage, but the incident was recorded on the daily casualties list at Lloyds.

Each of *Queen Mary*'s anchors weighed 16 tons, and each link of chain was 2 feet (60 cm) long.

Another near-miss occurred in January 1949. The ship had anchored in Cherbourg Harbour to collect passengers before heading for New York. As preparations were made to depart, the starboard anchor became entangled with something on the seabed. Several attempts were made to break free, but without success. The cause of the difficulty was the redundant PLUTO line (Pipe Line Under The Ocean), used to supply Allied forces with fuel during the Second World War. Weather conditions worsened as a Force Seven wind blew up, and so Captain Harry Grattidge lowered the port anchor. The ship was saved from drifting on to rocks, but she was aground. This was a problematic situation: within a few hours the tide would be out and there was a real danger that the ship's back would break. Crew worked through the night with cutters and by 7:00 am next morning the ship was free from her anchor. By now the tide had dropped by nearly 20 feet (6 metres) and *Queen Mary*'s propellers were out of the water.

The severity of the damage could not be judged while at sea; with the morning tide the liner was afloat again. *Queen Mary* was taken back to Southampton and drydocked for inspection. It was a narrow escape: the grounding had occurred between the two forward propellers, one of the strongest parts of the keel. Damage was limited to leaking rivets and dented plates. As a temporary repair 60 tons of cement were poured into the ship around the damage, and the voyage to New York was resumed.

62 ■ How many tugs were needed to manoeuvre *Queen Mary* in and out of port?

A ship the size of *Queen Mary* would usually have at least four tugs in attendance as a matter of routine when berthing, but there were very rare occasions when she berthed unaided. Famously, in February 1953 a tugboat strike meant that there were no boats available to dock the liner. Cunard had a strict schedule to maintain and so Relief Captain Donald Sorrell, in charge of the ship for only the second time, was wired to ask if he could berth without tugs. It was a tall order. The ship's driving gear was designed to deliver 160,000 shaft horsepower for long distances, not for manoeuvering around in port, and the Hudson River has strong currents which made the task more hazardous. But, against the advice of the local pilot, Captain Sorrell agreed. As the ship neared its berth at Pier 90 the Captain produced a homemade sighting tool, constructed from a wood block and nails. Using the instrument Sorrell shouted orders from the bridge wing to the Quartermaster, Ken Furr, who was at

Captain Donald Sorrell on the bridge of *Queen Mary*. One of 33 captains to be master of the ship, he took command in August 1952.

An officer looks out from the starboard bridge wing, which provided a commanding view of the ship forward and looking aft.

Tugs help to manoeuvre *Queen Mary* through Southampton's docks on an early post-war voyage.

the helm. Two of the ship's propellers were used to slowly edge the vessel closer. All seemed well. Then without warning the current caught the stern, pushing it closer to the pier. The bow immediately swung out towards West Highway, sending a scared crowd of onlookers fleeing, and Sorrell ordered 'All astern'. In the nick of time disaster was averted and the Captain prepared for a second attempt. He was successful and his achievement was reported around the world the following day.

63 ■ Did *Queen Mary* carry cargo?

In addition to passengers' personal luggage and sacks of mail there was space for freight. Deck plans from 1936 indicate areas at the forward end of F Deck were used for 'Motor Cars or Cargo'. There was, in fact, space to 'garage' up to 36 cars, and although motoring was in its relative infancy, some of the more wealthy passengers made use of the service and took vehicles to the

Queen Mary's searchlights were among the most powerful fitted to a ship when first installed. They were used to help guide the vessel through fog and mist, and also for signalling.

United States. Over the years *Queen Mary* had some interesting articles of cargo logged, including consignments of gold and silver: in 1964 one shipment of silver alone comprised 600 bars. And among the more unusual items, the ship also transported a replacement propeller for *Saxonia* (1954) another ship of the Cunard fleet, a private stable of horses, and a consignment of over 10,000 lb (4,536 kg) of heavy water bound for the Atomic Energy Commission in Britain.

64 ▓ Is it true RMS *Queen Mary* is haunted?

Over the decades there have been various sightings. Several of the alleged visits from the spirit world are re-occurring. The most convincing stories are associated with real events, such as the ghost of an 18-year old crewman who was with colleagues in the engine room when bells rang signalling a routine test of watertight doors. It was reported that, for reasons unknown, he tried to pass through the doorway at the last moment. He didn't make it. The heavy door slid closed and the young seaman was killed. His ghost has apparently appeared at the spot on a number of occasions. Another popular story features the ghost of a woman, this time a passenger, who drowned in the First Class Swimming Pool. In the eerie atmosphere of the now disused, dimly lit pool it's easy to understand why accounts like this are given credibility. Among the many other recorded apparitions is Winston Churchill. The British Prime Minister travelled aboard a number of times during the 1940s and '50s. More recently, claims of cigar smoke and various noises have been reported emanating from the First Class cabin on A Deck that he used to frequent.

Are the sightings fact or fiction? The answer will probably never be known. A number of those who have experienced a sighting are adamant they have witnessed the paranormal, but many, many more people have worked in the darkest, remotest areas of the ship for years without ever encountering anything out of the ordinary.

As troop-carrier *Queen Mary* set a new record for the greatest number of passengers carried on a single voyage (top). When approaching New York during the war, the ship is met by escort vessels and an anti-submarine blimp (below).

The War Years

65 ■ Where was the ship when the Second World War began?

When news came that Britain was officially at war *Queen Mary* was at sea on an eastbound voyage heading for New York with a full complement of passengers. The passenger list was largely filled with American citizens returning to the United States to avoid hostilities. In response to the news, the ship was immediately put on Full War Alert. This meant all deck lights were left off at night, extra lookouts were posted and a prescribed 'zig-zag' course was begun as a precaution against possible submarine attack. And crew were ordered to black out all 2,000 of the ship's portholes and windows.

Bob Hope and his wife Dolores were aboard when war was declared.

The War Alert activities were a tangible reminder of the potential danger threatening *Queen Mary*'s passengers. It was an anxious time. In the event the ship made it safely to New York and berthed at Pier 90 as usual on 4 September 1939. It was unclear at this point what would become of the ship. Cunard requested she should be regarded as a ship of peace, other parties called for her to be requisitioned and put to work, some thought her just too big a target to travel, and extremists suggested the ship be scrapped and the steel used in the war effort. The wrangling went on for six months.

66 ■ What were her wartime duties?

It is not unusual for ships of the merchant navy to be requisitioned and converted for different roles during times of war. Liners such as *Canberra* and *QE2*, ferries and other merchant vessels played a significant part as recently as the Falkland's War in 1982. During the Second World War the new breed of 'superliner' came into its own. *Queen Mary*'s tremendous speed capability and capacity were undeniable. In March 1940 Britain's Ministry of Shipping finally requisitioned the liner officially. A new chapter was begun. *Queen Mary* was about to become a troop-carrier. It was a role that would see her carry nearly a million soldiers, voyage into waters she would never normally enter, and steam over 650,000 miles.

British Prime Minister Winston Churchill was amongst the ship's wartime passengers. He travelled under the name Colonel Warden on several occasions, and on one North Atlantic crossing first reviewed plans for the D-Day invasion. Churchill later stated that he believed *Queen Mary* and her sister-ship *Queen Elizabeth* (which also undertook similar war duties), shortened the Second World War by at least a year: 'Vital decisions depended on their ability to continuously elude the enemy and without their aid the day of final victory must unquestionably have been postponed.'

67 ■ What changes were made in preparation for the ship's wartime role?

Before *Queen Mary* could leave port, she was painted from top to bottom, including over her name, in camouflage grey. On 21 March 1940 the 'Grey Ghost', as *Queen Mary* became affectionately known, left New York for Sydney, Australia, where the first phase of conversion would take place. The lavish furniture and fittings of First Class were removed, along with various objet d'art and paintings. Artwork that formed part of the fabric of the ship and couldn't be removed was, where possible, boarded over and protected. Extra bunks were fitted to provide accommodation for around 5,000 troops, more than double her peacetime capacity, and a sonar system designed to detect submarines was installed. Unfortunately this didn't function properly due to the noise of the ship's four huge propellers. In addition, armaments were fitted: a 6-inch (15-cm) gun at the ship's stern and anti-aircraft guns in various positions. An electronic 'degaussing strip' was also added virtually all the way around the outside of the hull between B and C decks. This was an effective precaution against magnetic mines. In the right light a faint outline of where it once lay can still be seen.

68 What was life on board like for the troops?

Queen Mary's first voyage as troop-carrier came on 4 May 1940. She left Australia with approximately 5,000 Australian and New Zealand troops bound for Britain. In spite of the ship being one of the largest, fastest and most prestigious in the world, the trip was gruelling. *Queen Mary* was designed for the cooler North Atlantic climate and so, with the exception of a few public areas, lacked air conditioning. The intense heat caused rioting and a number of deaths from heat exhaustion. Later in the voyage, when the ship called at Simonstown in Africa for refuelling, hundreds of troops went AWOL.

As the war progressed troops were urgently needed in different areas of the world. After the attack on Pearl Harbour in 1941, American troops were carried south to defend Australia. By now the ship's schedule was under the military control of the United States, but the British captain and crew remained. The liner's capacity was further increased in stages until she was able to accommodate over 15,000 troops, around six times her intended number of berths.

Extra toilet facilities were added and tiered berths called 'Standee bunks' were squeezed into every available space, including the luxury First Class swimming pool, which was drained and fitted with bunks seven high. Elsewhere men slept in groups of up to 21 in First Class staterooms originally intended for two people. Maintaining a tight ship was essential. With so many aboard even the most mundane activities became a logistical nightmare. Men slept in shifts around the clock, a practice that became known as 'hot-bunking', and the galley produced over 30,000 meals each day. The First Class Restaurant was packed with long trestle tables and turned into the main mess hall for the duration. There was no shortage of food, but conditions were extremely cramped with tightly packed crowds of men everywhere. It was often hard even to find a place to sit. Although gambling was high on a list of prohibited activities, poker games with very high stakes became a favourite way to pass the time.

69 ■ Were conditions just as cramped for officers?

For officers conditions were very different. They were served in their own mess by 'mess boys' in white jackets and enjoyed refinements such as table linen, silverware and menus. In addition, their sleeping arrangements were altogether better than their troops': in some cases six senior officers would share a stateroom, with the added luxury of their own generously proportioned bathroom. Officers enjoyed a little more privacy than lower ranks, but throughout the ship stateroom doors were removed, for fear they might jam in a heavy explosion.

70 ■ What was the greatest number of troops carried?

During the latter part of the war *Queen Mary* settled into a regular pattern of transatlantic passages known as the 'GI Shuttle'. On one of these voyages, in July 1943, the liner carried an incredible 15,740 troops and crew of 943, a total of 16,683 people. It set a new record for the most people ever carried by ship on a single voyage. The record remains unbroken to this day.

71 ■ Did the ship ever engage the enemy or suffer casualties?

The gun crews on *Queen Mary* were drilled and put through their paces every daylight watch and occasionally during night watches. Training in weapon handling and signalling was given to temporary gunners, and escort planes were used to practice lining up anti-aircraft guns. The ship and her crew were kept in a state of readiness for attack, but an attack never came and the ship's armaments were never fired in anger. However, in October 1942 there occurred the greatest tragedy in the liner's history. On the last leg of a voyage from the United States to Gourock in Scotland, *Queen Mary* was met by a small flotilla of Royal Naval vessels assigned to escort the ship across the Irish Sea. The task of guarding the liner-turned-troopship against attack from the air was given to the 4,290-ton light cruiser HMS *Curacoa* (1918). The cruiser had a maximum speed capability of 25 knots and her master, Captain Boutwood, knew the liner would overtake his vessel. He signalled to Captain Illingworth of *Queen Mary* his intention to: '…edge in astern of you'. Less than two hours later the two vessels collided. People aboard *Queen Mary* felt no more than a bump, but *Curacoa* was sliced in half as the liner ploughed through her, and 329 of the 430 crew were lost.

Queen Mary's bow was severely damaged, but she was able to continue her course to Gourock at reduced speed. After temporary repairs enabling an Atlantic crossing, a new stem section was fitted in the United States' Naval drydock at Boston. The whole incident was hidden under a veil of secrecy until after the war. The most likely cause was found to be interaction between the two ships, which pulled the cruiser into the liner's path.

72 ■ How did the Axis Powers view *Queen Mary*?

The *Queen* liners were incredibly big targets. Sinking either one of them could effectively amount to destroying or capturing a whole division of troops. The propaganda value alone would have been immense. Consequently, the incentive to sink them was huge. Adolf Hitler promised

U-boat captains Germany's highest military decoration, the Knights Cross of the Iron Cross with Oak Leaves, and a financial prize equivalent to a quarter of a million dollars. But the 'Grey Ghost' was too fast for them. She could sustain speeds in excess of 30 knots for thousands of miles, and could even outrun the earlier torpedoes.

Queen Mary's closest shave with the enemy occurred when a Nazi spy was found to have reported the liner's intended route and time of departure. The ship's master, Captain Bisset, left port ahead of schedule and immediately changed course. But the Axis Powers were so sure of their information they announced on public radio that *Queen Mary* had been destroyed. On hearing the news Captain Bisset commented: 'Keep it under your hat – don't let the troops know we've been sunk, it might worry them!'

73 ■ What happened immediately after the war?

Queen Mary made her last troopship voyage of the war in March 1945. The vessel was then drydocked for several weeks stateside and was, in fact, still in New York alongside *Queen Elizabeth* when news came of the Allied victory in Europe. The *Queen*s' sirens roared across the harbour in a chorus of celebration with local ships. But *Queen Mary*'s war duties were far from over. The following month the ship's company had the honour of taking the first American units home. The ecstatic greeting the ship received in the Hudson River rivalled her inaugural reception nearly a decade earlier. And

thousands of well-wishers turned out to welcome the liner as she arrived at her homeport of Southampton a few weeks later, after an absence of six years.

The last of her duties came during the following months as *Queen Mary* repatriated further United States person-nel and transported 22,000 GI brides from Britain and Europe to start new lives in North America. Four babies were even born en route.

After the war Queen Mary took 22,000 GI brides and their children to the United States.

The ship was finally decommissioned as troop-carrier in September 1946. Work on re-converting her for commercial use could begin at last.

74 ■ How long did the post-war conversion take?

The task of turning the two Cunard war veterans back into prestigious luxury liners was vast. *Queen Elizabeth* was refitted while laying at anchor in the Firth of Clyde in Scotland, but work on *Queen Mary* was undertaken at Southampton in the King George V drydock. Fifteen hundred workers were drafted in from Clydeside and housed in a camp outside the port. Around 10,000 pieces of furniture were taken out of stores in Britain, America and Australia, dusted-off and refurbished. On board, the ship's woodwork was renovated. Over the years thousands of GIs had added their initials to the handrails around the ship. A small section was kept as a tribute to those who lost their lives, but most were sanded away. Elsewhere, 120 French polishers were kept busy restoring interior wood panelling. Staterooms were also restored, and given new carpet and furnishings. But the refit was much more

A 10-month post-war refit was carried out in Southampton, during which further work to her stem was carried out following her collision with HMS *Curacoa* (see question 71).

With the anti-mine degaussing strip removed, wartime grey is over-painted with Cunard's familiar black, white and red livery.

than cosmetic. Cunard took the chance to make major changes, including building a First Class air-conditioned cinema with capacity for 200 people. And First and Second Class Garden Lounges were fitted on the Promenade Deck, one each side of the ship. A similar room aboard *Queen Elizabeth* had already proved very popular.

Additionally, artwork was restored and new pieces commissioned. Many of the artists who contributed to the ship's original fitting-out were now part of a huge restoration team.

Mechanically *Queen Mary* was given a very thorough overhaul. Her propellers were removed and shafts drawn out. A completely new stem was fitted, and 3,000 gallons of anti-fouling paint applied to the hull. The 10-month long refit restored, remodelled and transformed *Queen Mary* in readiness for the two-ship weekly service conceived twenty years earlier.

Queen Mary is inspected at her homeport at the beginning of a new season.

End of an Era

75 ■ Why were the *Queen* liners taken out of service?

The idea of two giant passenger ships capable of providing a weekly transatlantic service was first conceived in the late 1920s. The two-ship operation of *Queen Mary* and sistership *Queen Elizabeth* came into effect only after the Second World War, yet it proved a very successful partnership, with Cunard dominating the North Atlantic trade for ten years. Early passenger aircraft offered limited competition, but as long-range planes were developed, the jet age dawned. More and more travellers opted for a few hours in the air rather than four-and-a-half days at sea, especially in winter months when crossings could be rough and uncomfortable.

By 1957 the airlines had won half the transatlantic market. Passenger numbers were falling alarmingly. The crew often outnumbered passengers two-to-one and within a decade the ship went from returning a handsome profit to losing nearly £15,000 each week. Something had to be done, and so in 1967 *Queen Mary* was sold and retired to the sun (see question 77).

76 ■ Was the ship ever used for cruising?

Queen Mary was originally intended for line voyaging only, but during the burgeoning tourist trade in the early 1960s cruising was introduced to generate extra income. The first *Queen Mary* cruise, a six-day Christmas excursion to Las Palmas, left Southampton on 23 December 1963. New York became the embarkation for cruises to locations such as the Bahamas, and in early 1966 a month-long tour of the Mediterranean called at Madeira, Lisbon, Gibraltar, Palma, Cannes, Naples, Piraeus, Tangier and Las Palmas. Some changes were introduced for *Queen Mary*'s cruising role. The Second Class Lounge became the Flamenco Room, with bright colours, trellis and striped awnings above fake windows obscuring 1930s panelling and artwork. And the forward Observation Lounge, traditional hot-spot for First Class passengers, became an extension of Third Class. But, too large to traverse the Suez or Panama canals, and without adequate air conditioning, Cunard's *Queen*s were never to repeat their liner successes as 'cruisers'.

News of Cunard's plans to withdraw the *Queen* liners came on 9 May 1967. Their demise may have been inevitable but the announcement was still very much a surprise. *Queen Mary* had received a £1 million refit just months earlier and *Queen Elizabeth* had been expected to carry on for another five years at least. The important question of what to do with two uneconomic relics from a past era now had to be answered. Cunard did not want anyone else to operate *Queen Mary* as an ocean-going liner. Finding a new operator wouldn't have been easy but if successful the old ship effectively would have competed against Cunard's new superstar *QE2*. The alternatives were limited: sell *Queen Mary* for scrap or to an organisation that would not be taking her to sea. Offers poured in, varying from realistic to ridiculous.

In the end the city of Long Beach in California secured a deal with a bid of £1.23 million ($3.45 million) and a plan to turn the ship into a museum,

Thousands of New Yorkers come to bid the great ship farewell on her final departure from New York.

conference centre and hotel. Cunard offered to deliver *Queen Mary* to Long Beach at the city's expense using a skeleton crew. However, Long Beach officials had other ideas. They wanted *Queen Mary* to make a triumphant arrival brimming with excitable passengers. And so the ship's voyage to retirement was sold by Furgazy Travel of New York as her 'Last Great Cruise'. The 39-day excursion was to be her longest peacetime voyage. The liner would steam nearly 15,000 miles, around Cape Horn, would cross the equator twice and sail through the Tropics. The ship departed Southampton for the very last time on 31 October 1967, arriving in Long Beach on 9 December.

78 ■ How many people came to see the ship's last departure?

When the day finally arrived for *Queen Mary* to depart English shores for the last time, the story gripped the interest of the national and international media. After over thirty years in service *Queen Mary* was far more than just another ship; for some the liner was their source of employment, for others part of the cityscape and a way of life. The ship's final departure was emotional. An estimated 200,000 people crowded vantage points along the shores of Southampton Water to

As *Queen Mary* left Southampton for the very last time, she received a special radiogram message from Captain Marr of *Queen Elizabeth*.

witness the moment; each of the port's dock cranes nodded in salute as the ship passed; and 14 Royal Navy helicopters flew overhead in an anchor formation. At the head of her main mast *Queen Mary* flew her paying-off pennant, which was 310 feet in length, 10 feet for every year at sea. As strains of 'Auld Lang Syne' faded from ashore, and the flotilla of tugs and pleasure craft fell away, *Queen Mary* made her final departure. History was made and an era ended.

79 ■ What was it like aboard for the 'Last Great Cruise'?

The response to the farewell cruise was a surprise. Even before the first advertisement there were 500 bookings and in the event the ship sailed with 1,093 passengers. The itinerary included seven ports, which would be crucial for refuelling. The average speed was reduced to around 20 knots and two of the ship's engines and boilers were closed down, reducing fuel consumption by half. As the ship entered warmer waters, the age-old problem of heat became apparent. Many passengers without air-conditioned staterooms found the heat unbearable. The problem was so severe that crewmember Leonard Horsburgh collapsed and died, and was buried at sea.

In spite of the discomfort most passengers had an enjoyable time on the

Dutch Miller swims in the First Class pool while the ship rounds Cape Horn.

final cruise. Excursions were available at each port and entertainment was provided by artists including Tessie O'Shea, the Meyer Davis Orchestra and Johnny Mathis. Even during this last voyage *Queen Mary* was entering the record books, becoming the first (and last) three-funnelled liner to round Cape Horn. As the ship laid claim to the record, Dutch Miller swam laps in the First Class Swimming Pool, later claiming to be the only person in the world to have swum around Cape Horn. The voyage was also famous for some unusual cargo: two double-decker buses, intended for tourist use in Long Beach, were carried on the open Main Deck.

During the last ocean-going party aboard the liner, *Queen Mary*'s master, Captain John Treasure Jones, announced that as the ship went into retirement so too would he: 'This is the last night that I shall be addressing my passengers, so it's a rather sad night for me ... but I'm also very proud indeed and privileged to be captain of this ship on this last, historic cruise.'

80 ■ How did the people of Long Beach respond to *Queen Mary*?

The ship made the triumphant entrance for which Long Beach councillors had been hoping. The dawn sunlight of 9 December revealed around five hundred craft following the liner as she steamed the last leg of the voyage. The ship arrived in Long Beach to an overwhelming reception. A flotilla of 10,000 vessels, the largest armada since the evacuation of Dunkirk, came to greet *Queen Mary*, along with helicopters and a crowd of around a million people. Traffic on the water was so dense that on the ship's radar it appeared as a solid mass. Some small craft manoeuvred perilously close to the liner and called for souvenirs. In response, hundreds of items, from lifebelts to chairs and small tables, were hurled over the side. At 11:30 am the ship berthed and the signal 'Finished with engines' given by her captain for the last time.

81 ■ When did Long Beach Council take possession of the ship?

On 11 December, two days after *Queen Mary*'s arrival in California, a brief ceremony was held in the Verandah Grill. The ship was officially presented to the city of Long Beach and the British Ensign replaced by the 'Stars & Stripes'. Captain John Treasure Jones observed: 'I was captain of *Mauretania*. I took her to the breakers; bringing this ship here, at least means she will live.'

Queen Mary, in full regalia, makes a grand entrance on her arrival at Long Beach on 9 December 1967.

A flotilla of up to 10,000 small craft greets *Queen Mary* as she approaches Long Beach, each sounding its horn in welcome with the liner adding to the commotion in response.

82 ■ What happened to the ship immediately after arrival in America?

A condition of the sale stated that *Queen Mary* would no longer be a sea-going vessel and to ensure this was met one of the first tasks was to cut the ship's drive shafts, rendering her inoperable. Long Beach had big plans for their new acquisition, but before conversion work could begin the ship had to be drydocked at a nearby naval yard and made ready. While out of the water three of the four 35-ton propellers were removed, and 90 of the ship's 94 through-hull openings sealed. Stabiliser fins installed ten years earlier were removed, and the hull below the waterline sandblasted and painted with 3,000 gallons of anti-fouling paint. A steel box was constructed and welded to the side of the ship over the last remaining propeller. This was designed to provide visitors with a view of the screw slowly rotating in the water. On 17 May 1968 seven tugs guided *Queen Mary* from drydock and towards Pier E, where the full-scale conversion would get under way.

83 ■ What happened to the other superliners?

In the 1930s there were only two other ships that qualified as super-liners. The first was *Normandie* of France, the largest liner in the world when launched in 1932, and the first over 1,000 feet (305 metres) in length. *Normandie* had a very glamorous and very brief career. Like *Queen Mary* she was requisitioned for war duties (in her case by the government of the United States). In February 1942 the ship was undergoing conversion to troop-carrier at her berth in New York when fire broke out. In spite of warnings from her architect Vladimir Yourkevitch, who was on the quayside, the Fire Department pumped so much water aboard that the ship

Captain John Treasure Jones gives the signal 'Finished with Engines' for the very last time (above). Alongside passengers, two double-decker buses were also carried to Long Beach.

BLACK & WHITE is big on flavour

Captain John Treasure Jones presents the liner's flags to Mayor Wade of Long Beach.

became unstable and capsized. Plans to rebuild her were eventually abandoned and in 1947 the rusting hulk of *Normandie* was scrapped.

The other great superliner was *Queen Elizabeth*, sistership to *Queen Mary*. The 'Lizzie' went into service at the beginning of the Second World War and immediately joined her sister as troop-carrier. After the war she was refitted and entered service as a North Atlantic liner as intended. *Queen Elizabeth* was highly successful and with a length of 1,031 feet (314 metres) and gross tonnage of 83,000 tons, she was largest liner in the world. Like *Queen Mary*, the ship was withdrawn from service and sold in the late 1960s. Eventually, after a second change of ownership, she became *Seawise University*, a mobile centre of study that would travel the world. The ship was refitted and prepared for her new role but in January 1971 she was set alight and sank in Hong Kong Harbour. The subsequent enquiry discovered that fires had been started in various locations simultaneously and gave a verdict of 'sabotage by person or persons unknown'.

In her new stationary role *Queen Mary*'s vast anchor chains, each with a total length of 990 feet (302 metres), would be redundant, but lengths remained on board along with the 16-ton anchors.

Queen Mary in the US naval drydock in Long Beach for prelimina conversion work in 1968. The dock is less than half a mile (800 metres) from Pier E, where the ship berthed on arrival.

A New Beginning

84 ■ How much did it cost to convert *Queen Mary* to a visitor attraction?

Only one day after the ship had arrived in Long Beach illustrations were released that unveiled the plans for *Queen Mary*. The centrepiece was to be a Museum of the Sea, to include elaborate displays and a 360-degree motion picture screen. The space below R Deck, extending to the hold and to include the engine and boiler rooms, would accommodate the new oceanarium, and a separate exhibition, the engine-room catwalk, would take visitors around a massive turbine and gearbox. The covers were to be removed so that the 'working' machinery was visible, and a new window below the waterline would allow a view of one of the ship's propellers slowly turning. It was an ambitious project. The estimated cost was $8.5 million, including the purchase of the ship, not a high price for extensive conversion of a vessel that had cost three times as much to build over thirty years before. A few months later local newspapers reported an increase in budget to $14 million; after a year the figure had become $32 million. The actual cost was over $100 million for a conversion much less extensive than originally planned.

85 ■ Who paid for the conversion?

Long Beach officials, enthused by the idea of acquiring the old Cunarder as a local landmark, originally tried to persuade businesses in the private sector to finance the acquisition and conversion of the ship. When this failed an alternative means of funding had to be found. Millions of dollars were held in the Tideland Oil Trust, money paid to the city for the right to exploit local oilfields. A significant sum had been earmarked for the building of a Museum of the Sea, and so it was argued that if the museum were sited within the ship, Tideland money could be used legitimately to finance the project. Further money was raised in the form of investment by concession-aires, and $286,000 generated by auctioning surplus items included in the purchase of *Queen Mary*, such as 375 waste baskets, 1,000 deckchairs, 50,000 napkins and more than 83,000 tea bags.

Over 20,000 tons of unwanted machinery and fittings were removed from the liner and sold for scrap, including drive shafts, boilers, turbines and the electrical generating room.

86 ■ How long did the Long Beach conversion take?

For a variety of reasons the process of adapting *Queen Mary* for her new career suffered many delays. Difficulties with labour relations, mistakes and unforeseen complications meant that the project took four years, four times longer than initially hoped.

87 ■ What work was done?

While the ship was being prepared in drydock plans for the conversion were revised and extended. French oceanographer Jacques Cousteau was appointed consultant to the Museum of the Sea; the area assigned to the museum was increased by forty per cent and the opening date set for autumn 1969. Work needed to be completed in less than a year to meet the deadline, but the revamp was still at the planning stage. Details of the size of the project began to emerge: the liner's original 1,200 cabins were to be replaced by 400 larger staterooms, she would be re-wired throughout, re-carpeted, and air conditioning was to be installed. To accommodate the new oceanarium areas below decks would change beyond all recognition. Unwanted mechanical components, two complete decks at the aft end of the ship and 23 bulkheads were removed. Around 20,000 tons of steel and other materials were hauled out through funnel hatches and sold for scrap. Beams and columns were installed to make the structure safe, and escalators were fitted to link the various levels, ready for exhibits.

During the process of remodelling a variety of original rooms disappeared, among them the Second Class Swimming Pool, First Class Cinema and Gymnasium, and crew quarters. It was a slow process, and the opening date was delayed until the summer of 1970. A few months later the estimated cost rose again from $32 million to $57 million and the opening postponed again until December. The local population was growing increasingly impatient, exacerbated by continued negative press coverage. Even County Supervisor Kenneth Hahn referred to the project as 'a monument to stupidity'.

The Museum of the Sea, however, was nearing completion on time, although with only a third of its intended exhibits. The remainder were rescheduled until after opening. Externally, crews battled to meet deadlines. *Queen Mary*'s hull and superstructure were sandblasted and 320 tons of paint

Vast spaces were created below decks to house the 'Museum of the Sea' project, which was to include a rotating tower and a monorail.

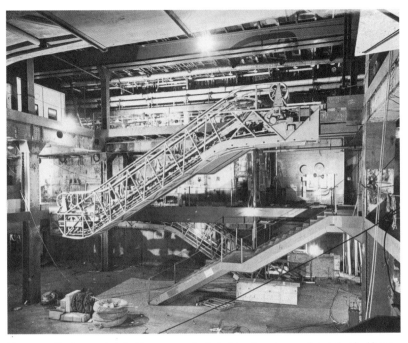

New strengthening was installed to compensate for bulkheads and areas of deck that had been removed, and escalators were added to link decks.

removed, causing the liner to raise 1½ inches (4 cm) in the water. New funnels were constructed and installed, and eight tons of paint were applied, returning the ship to her original Cunard colours of black hull, white super-structure, and black-topped red funnels.

There was still much to be done, but on 27 February 1971 the ship made her last voyage as she was manoeuvred from Pier E to her new permanent berth at Pier J; a distance of 4½ miles (7.25 km). British-born actress Greer Garson ceremonially tied a mooring line before a crowd of 60,000 people. On 8 May preview tours began: *Queen Mary* was at last open to the public.

The Museum of the Sea made a very bold statement. It included a rotating themed tower five decks high and even a monorail to transport visitors from one part to another. However, the museum was never completed and was eventually closed and withdrawn. Cavernous areas below decks, which were cleared to make way for the later phases of the museum, lay bare much as contractors left them in the 1960s. A poignant message of farewell, hastily chalked on a bulkhead by crew, remains to this day in a forgotten recess.

88 ■ Why were the funnels replaced?

When the funnels were removed to gain access to the shafts they proved to be in very poor condition. Portions crumbled as they were placed on the quay beside the ship. They were literally held together in places by 105 coats of paint applied over the decades, which formed a film ⁵⁄₁₆ inch (8 mm) thick. Replacement steel funnels were built, each comprising a 6-feet (1.8-metre) high base ring, weighing one ton, and four further sections of six tons. Each component was carefully craned into position. The replacement stacks are slightly smaller than the originals, and welded together rather than riveted as they were in the 1930s.

89 ■ What happened to the Verandah Grill?

During preparations for new restaurants aboard, the Verandah Grill was all but gutted. No longer a luxurious resort of the rich and famous, it became a fast-food outlet. This aspect of the conversion was greatly criticised by enthusiasts, historians and former passengers and crew. It remained that way for

The legendary Verandah Grill, one of the most famous public spaces on board, has now been fully restored after spending many years as a fast-food outlet.

years until the RMS Foundation took steps to reverse the process. The outlet was removed and the room redecorated. For some time it was used in this state as a function room, but towards the end of the 1990s further work was completed. The original period fittings and the artwork produced by Doris Zinkeisen, which had been stored deep below decks, were retrieved and the Verandah Grill was finally restored to its former glory.

90 ■ What did the press make of the delayed opening and rise in costs?

The arrival of *Queen Mary* made headlines, and certainly put Long Beach on the map. This was exactly what city officials had hoped, but as events unfolded much of the press coverage became extremely damning. George Reasons wrote a comprehensive report for the *Los Angeles Times* in which he alleged that poor management and lack of planning had plagued the project. In 1971 Reasons wrote:

> Three entities were independently at work on the vessel: the city, Diners Queen Mary and the Museum of the Sea.
> When one changed plans, it produced a domino effect throughout the ship.
> Long Beach created a special *Queen Mary* Department, with a staff of 91 employees to co-ordinate the work, but the job proved too much for them.'

The report went on to describe an alleged catalogue of blunders and mis-calculations that added significantly to the delay and cost of the project. In spite of this and other negative articles the public remained enthusiastic, although impatient; even if some individuals had reservations, the city council remained committed and acknowledged that the future of Long Beach depended on the success of the ship.

91 ■ Was the project a success?

During the first weekend that *Queen Mary* was open for business 17,000 people toured the ship, assisted by 65 guides. Thousands more were turned away. City officials were delighted by the response. Within five months 650,000 people had passed through the gates, generating over $500,000. When the Museum of the Sea opened in December 1971 it attracted 4,000 people on the first day alone. During the first year of trading *Queen Mary* the attraction received 1.5 million visitors, who spent around $6.5 million.

Even larger numbers were predicted for the following 12 months and thousands of advanced hotel bookings were taken. In January 1973 Hotel Queen Mary officially opened its doors. First Class staterooms had been sympathetically brought up to date, while retaining a substantial amount of original materials and design, and new rooms were constructed in areas previously occupied by Second or Third Class accommodation. The following month a new record for visitor numbers was set. Nearly 40,000 people toured the ship during a three-day holiday weekend. The vessel was living up to the commercial hopes and dreams of councillors. The project was a success.

But success was short-lived. A few weeks later it was revealed the Museum of the Sea wasn't paying its way. Industrial unrest was brewing between the company running the hotel operation and their employees. And allegations also appeared in the press of the illegal use of $14 million of Tideland Oil Fund money. Council officials denied the alleged claims, but the issue did nothing to enhance the reputation of the financially faltering *Queen Mary*. For numerous reasons, for much of the next two decades the project fell short of council expectations. Operators came and went, including the Disney Corporation, who decided not to renew their lease when it expired in 1992.

Long Beach was left with a dilemma: should the city cut its losses and dispose of the ship or remain committed to finding a way to make the project work? Tenders to buy *Queen Mary* were invited and, just as in 1967, they arrived from around the world. But campaigners in Long Beach fought to keep the ship. In the end, councillors voted unanimously to retain the liner. *Queen Mary* was once again reprieved, and a new operator appointed. The RMS Foundation under the direction of Joseph Prevratil took over the vessel's management in February 1993.

Retirement in the sun:
RMS *Queen Mary* today
(Author)

Queen Mary today

92 ■ Is the ship in concrete?

Many people think the old liner is in drydock; some have even heard that she is set in concrete. This is a myth that has been perpetuated in print over the years. In fact, *Queen Mary* is floating, raised and lowered gently by the tide at her permanent berth. In a very real sense she is a ship. But as far as the Long Beach authorities are concerned *Queen Mary* is now a building. The liner no longer goes anywhere and she is reliant on facilities ashore for all her power, water and sanitation.

93 ■ What condition is the ship in today?

Since Cunard Line sold the vessel she has hit the headlines periodically. Unfortunately, this was not always for the right reasons. Concern over the condition of the ship below the waterline has regularly been the subject of speculation. In the early 1990s, when *Queen Mary* was for sale, there were a number of particularly negative press reports suggesting that the liner might sink at her berth any moment. The City Council commissioned a thorough independent survey of the hull. The results were very positive and established that the ship was in 'great shape'. A system installed to inhibit corrosion has proven to be extremely effective.

94 ■ Did I see *Queen Mary* in *Diagnosis Murder*?

It wasn't long before nearby Hollywood realised the potential for using the old liner as a ready-made film set. Since the 1970s *Queen Mary* has featured in over 300 movies, television programmes (including *Diagnosis Murder*) and commercials, occasionally as herself but more often as a fictitious luxury liner or anonymous Art Deco interior. Becoming a film location has provided an effective way to generate extra income.

One of the first productions to use the ship as a location was *The Poseidon Adventure* (1972) starring Gene Hackman. The film was based on Paul Gallico's best selling novel, in which a liner is capsized by a freak wave. By chance, the author was inspired to write the book after sailing from Southampton aboard *Queen Mary* in 1937. He recalled:

In her present state *Queen Mary* relies on facilities ashore for power, water and sanitation: a world away from the days when she was all but self-sufficient. *(Author)*

We were at lunch when a particularly large trio of waves tried to climb over the Mary's stern. The old girl, in her anguish to escape, lay over on her side and, for what could be no more than a few seconds but seemed like years, stayed there. I can still see the dining room stewards bracing themselves against the incredible slant of the floor.

95 ■ Can the public see the ship's interior?

Queen Mary is open to the public for guided and self-guided tours. Unless private functions are taking place, most former First Class public areas of the ship are accessible. The Promenade, Sun and Sports decks are largely unrestricted, and much of the former First Class accommodation forms Hotel Queen Mary (see question 91).

96 ■ Is the ship in the right place?

There are people who think *Queen Mary* should never have been sold to an American city, especially a city on the west coast with no previous connection with the ship. People of Clydebank can justly lay claim to *Queen Mary*.

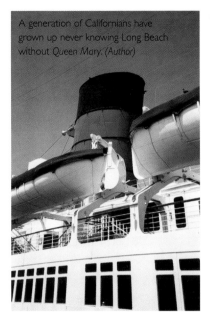

A generation of Californians have grown up never knowing Long Beach without *Queen Mary*. *(Author)*

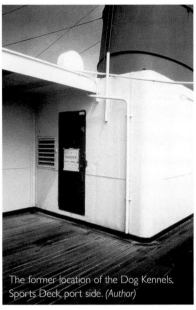

The former location of the Dog Kennels, Sports Deck, port side. *(Author)*

Queen Mary has now been an 'attraction' far longer than ever she was a working liner. *(Author)*

So, too, can the inhabitants of Southampton. Decades later, Long Beach has just as strong a case. The liner has spent many more years in retirement than in service, and a generation of local people have grown up never knowing the city without her. They hold *Queen Mary* in affection much like former passengers and crew, and take as much pride in her as the British. More importantly, the continuing success of *Queen Mary* is a question of stewardship rather than location or ownership. Like a rare piece of art, the ship is so historically significant on an international scale that her global position is no longer important. In fact, weather conditions in

The Windsor Salon, currently used as a function room, was created during the conversion by decking over the redundant central funnel hatch at R Deck. *(Author)*

California are much more favourable to a retired steel ship than in many other parts of the world, so there is no reason to believe that *Queen Mary* would be environmentally better served elsewhere.

97 ■ Would *Queen Mary* make more money if she were in Britain?

There is no definitive answer to this question because there are so many variables. It is true that *Queen Mary* has a checkered past since withdrawal from service, particularly in the early days, but this may well have been the case had the vessel remained in Europe. Other similar projects around the world have been met with limited success or failure, so relatively speaking, in spite of negative press reports from time to time, the ship is doing well.

98 ■ Could *Queen Mary* ever return to Southampton?

When the ship was converted in Long Beach during the late 1960s parts of the interior layout were substantially altered. Strengthening was put in place to make the ship safe for her new role, but she is no longer a sea-going vessel and is far from seaworthy. Other preparations like the removal of the

The former First Class Lounge today. These days the room is used for concerts, seminars and tea dances. *(Author)*

She may no longer be travelling the oceans, but *Queen Mary*'s Promenade Deck remains an evocative reminder of her sea-going days. *(Author)*

steel box over her last remaining propeller, and dismantling the substantial protective rock dyke around the ship would also have to be made. *Queen Mary* no longer has engines (see question 82), which would mean a journey around the notorious Cape Horn under tow. Although it is not impossible for her to return to Britain, it would be highly unlikely that the ship could survive such a long and hazardous journey. There are two other main considerations. Firstly, the finance: an exercise like this would cost tens of millions of pounds. Secondly, her availability: the City of Long Beach is proud to be custodian of the old ship and that is unlikely to change.

99 ■ What is the ship's role today?

In practical terms *Queen Mary* is a tourist attraction, hotel and exhibition and conference centre. Thousands visit the ship each year. Many are local people; others travel from far and wide specifically to see the liner. Various events are held on board throughout the year, from corporate conferences to public exhibitions, and local schools and colleges use *Queen Mary* as a venue for their end-of-year proms. Since her arrival at Long Beach a wedding chapel has been constructed on board the ship, which has proven popular. And every weekend a sumptuous buffet is held in the former First Class Restaurant:

Sunday Brunch has developed into something of a modern tradition aboard the ship. In theoretical terms *Queen Mary* is effectively a living museum, a place of education, and one of the best collections of Art Deco design to be found in the world.

100 ■ What might the future hold for the ship?

For a vessel built to withstand all the vagaries of the North Atlantic, life in peaceful retirement is altogether less demanding. One expert appointed to make regular checks of the hull beneath the waterline estimated the ship could carry on as she is for another 300 years. Although clearly good news, there is no room for complacency. *Queen Mary*'s operators are only too aware of how much money is required for maintenance, restoration and further development. During the 1990s a number of major restoration projects were carried out, such as reconditioning and sealing the teak decking and replacing the floor covering in Prom Deck Square with authentic materials. But there are still many more large- and small-scale restorations to be undertaken. There is always a job that needs to be done and costs that need to be met. There is also great potential (and plenty of space) to develop further displays and reconstructions reflecting life aboard during ocean-going days. Balancing historic integrity and commercial interest is not easy, but as long as people continue to visit the ship in significant numbers *Queen Mary* can build on previous successes and secure a bright future.

101 ■ Is *Queen Mary* still important?

Every time a liner from the 1930s or earlier has been lost or broken-up *Queen Mary*'s importance has grown. The ship has a distinctive place in history: first British 'superliner' over 1,000 feet (305 metres), a favourite of the rich and famous, impeccable war service a and long list of record achievements. These combine to create something very special: a ship that is unique. *Queen Mary* is the last superliner left in the world and it is essential that she continues to survive as the only tangible representative of liner travel of the past, for this and future generations. The ship's role has changed dramatically, but *Queen Mary* is as important today as ever.

Bibliography and Sources

Bowen, J., *Miniature Merchant Ships* (Conway Maritime Press, 1997)

Cunard, *The Fleet 1840–2004* (The Open Agency, 2004)

Dawson, P., *The Liner: Retrospective and Renaissance* (Conway Maritime Press, 2005)

Edington, S., *The Captain's Table* (National Maritime Museum, UK, 2005)

Ellery, D., *RMS Queen Mary, The World's Favourite Liner* (Waterfront Publications, 1994)

Greenway, A. (ed.), *The Golden Age of Shipping: The Classic Merchant Ship 1900–1960* (Conway Maritime Press, 1994)

Griffiths, D., *Steam at Sea: Two Centuries of Steam-Powered Ships* (Conway Maritime Press, 1997)

Hutchings, D., *RMS Queen Mary – 50 Years of Splendour* (Kingfisher Railway Productions, 1986)

Kelly, P., 'The Tragic Loss of HMS *Curacoa*' in *Warship* 1997–8 (Conway Maritime Press, 1998)

Maxtone-Graham, J., *The Only Way to Cross* (MacMillan, 1978)

Maxtone-Graham, J., *Cunard 150 Glorious Years* (David & Charles, 1989)

Miller, W. H., *Picture History of Queen Mary & Queen Elizabeth* (Dover Publications, 2004)

Steel, J., *Queen Mary* (Phaidon Press, 1995)

Watton, R., *The Cunard Liner Queen Mary – Anatomy of the Ship* series (Conway Maritime Press, 1989)

Original Sources

Madame Yevonde Portrait Archive (www.madameyevonde.com)

Marine Art Posters (www.marineartposters.co.uk)

Queen Mary Archive (not open for public research)

The Story of Queen Mary (souvenir publication, published 1936)

The Shipbuilder 'Queen Mary' (1936)

Southern Daily Echo Archive

Viewpoint Productions Archive (www.viewpoint-productions.co.uk)

Weekly Illustrated Special 'Queen Mary' Number (1936)

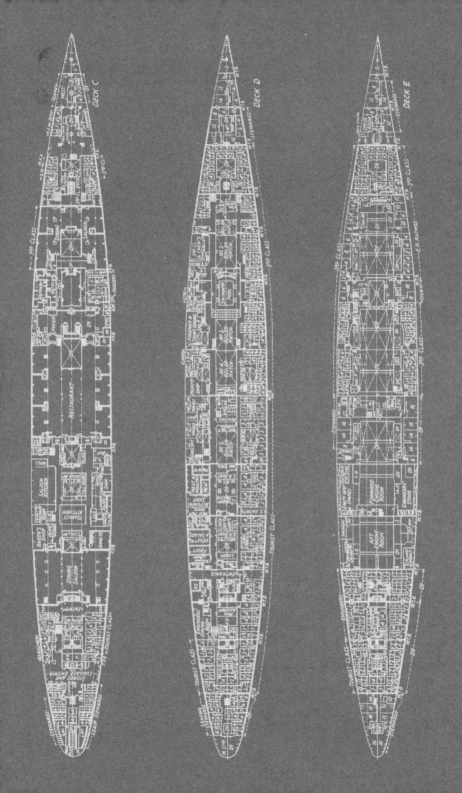